SEAPOWER

MODERN NAVAL TECHNOLOGY OF THE USA AND EUROPE

EDITED BY MI SEITELMAN · DESIGN BY DAVID POLEWSKI

First published in 1988 by Motorbooks International
Publishers & Wholesalers, Inc, P.O. Box 2, 729 Prospect Ave., Osceola, WI 54020 USA

© International Defense Images, 1988

Motorbooks International is a certified trademark
registered with the United States Patent Office

Printed and bound in Japan

The information in this book is true and complete to the
best of our knowledge. All recommendations are made without
any guarantee on the part of the authors or publisher, who
also disclaim any liability incurred in connection with the
use of this data or specific details.

Library of Congress Cataloging-in-Publication Data
Seapower, Modern Naval Technology of the USA and Europe

1. Navies 2. Seapower. I. International Defense Images (Firm)
VA10.54   1988   359   88-5309

ISBN 0-87938-304-6

Motorbooks International books are also available at discounts
in bulk quantity for industrial or sales-promotional use. For
details write to Special Sales Manager at the Publisher's Address

EDITORIAL STAFF

Susan Malinowski-Turner   Philip Farris   Gary Kieffer   Susan Mitchell

PHOTOGRAPHY

Mi Seitelman	Cover 1, 1-2, 55, 62-63, 93 center, 84-85, 94-96	John Lawlor	92, 93 top
		Joe Dobbels	USN, 12-13
		PA 2 Dan Vogeley	USCG, 44-45
Frederick Sutter	Cover 4, 46-47, 52-53, 90, 96	Tim Masterson	37 Center
		Tom Gillespie	49
Gary Kieffer	8 bottom, 88-89, 93 bottom, 95 top, bottom	Hans Halberstadt	48,50 bottom, center & right, 51 bottom
David Polewski	95 center		
Robin Adshead	24-33	Photos Courtesy Of:	
Kirby Harrison	36-37, 42-43	Martin Marietta, 5; Aerospatiale, 10-11, 14-15; British Aerospace, 16-17; Crenshaw International, 18-19; National Archives, 20-21; Fred Maroon, US Navy, 38-39; US Navy, 8-9, 34-35, 40-41, 56-57, 61, 66-67,82-83,86-87; US Coast Guard, 49 bottom, 50 top, bottom left, 51.	
Francois Guenet	68 thru 80		
Chuck Feil	58-59, 60, 64-65		
Chuck Mussi	22-23		

CONTENTS

USS IOWA (BB 61)

On the Cover
The USS HERCULES, PHM2, one of six
patrol combatant missile (hydrofoil) ships
of the U.S. Navy. **Photo by Mi Seitelman**

PROFILE: NORMAN R. AUGUSTINE DISCUSSES PRESSURES ON DEFENSE

By
J. Philip Geddes

Mr. Norman R. Augustine is the Vice-Chairman and Chief Executive Officer of Martin Marietta Corporation, a $5.2 billion, multi-faceted company with 70,000 employees, that makes a wide variety of defense systems. The aerospace/electronics part of Martin Marietta brings in roughly three quarters of total revenues, with the remaining quarter split between information systems and materials such as aggregates for the construction industry and refractories for steel making.

Martin Marietta has been singularly successful over recent months in acquiring new business, largely as a result of extraordinary investment in research and development focussed on bidding opportunities. This policy of sacrificing short term earnings, in what Mr. Augustine calls a "three year window of opportunity for long term growth," won large contracts for the national test bed for the Strategic Defense Initiative, the Air Defense Anti-Tank System (ADATS) for the Army, and the largest commercial space contract in history to launch 15 General Electric satellites on Titan commercial boosters.

Backlog at the end of 1987 stood at $10.8 billion and included a broad list of very different products with an order for 23 Air Force Titan IV launchers, the Magellan spacecraft for NASA, a huge production order for the LANTIRN electro-optic system for the Air Force's F-15s and F-16s, TADS/PVNS navigation and targeting systems for the AH-64 Apache helicopter, laser guidance for the HELLFIRE missile, COPPERHEAD laser designated artillery rounds, PATRIOT missile production under subcontract from Raytheon, vertical missile launchers for ships, and even a supersonic target for the Navy.

Martin Marietta's invest to win strategy brought in 48 percent of the programs and about 65 percent of the dollars bid on during the window of opportunity. This kind of performance makes it possible for Martin Marietta to grow during what Mr. Augustine describes as a declining market for defense over the next four or five years. On the minus side in the bidding game, Martin Marietta lost first place on NASA's space station and will inevitably not realize the original potential in the PERSHING II, as the nuclear intermediate range missiles are eliminated by the INF agreement with the Soviets.

Mr. Augustine (52) joined Martin Marietta in 1977 after serving as Under Secretary of the Army (1975-77). He was Assistant Secretary of the Army for Research and Development (1973-74). Mr. Augustine was made President and Chief Operating Officer of Martin Marietta in April 1986 and Vice-Chairman and Chief Executive Officer in December 1987, taking over as CEO from Chairman Thomas G. Pownall. Mr. Augustine has contributed to the founding of the Semiconductor Manufacturing Technology Institute (Sematech), a national consortium to develop high priority semiconductor devices.

Mr. Augustine speaks from experience on hostile takeovers having been with Martin Marietta during the successful counter attack led by Mr Pownall against the Bendix bid for Martin Marietta in 1982 that became known as the PacMan defense, in which the attacker gets attacked. Mr. Augustine's sagacity and broad wit are legend in an industry not known for its humor. Samples: "Sad to say, much of the planning conducted by American business has, as the old saying goes, made astrology look respectable," and on 'surrealistic' planning "... if today were half as good as tomorrow is supposed to be, it would probably be twice as good as yesterday was." And finally, "When it comes to acquisitions, there is good news and there is bad news. The bad news is that 75 percent of all acquisitions fail. The good news is 20 percent don't make any difference at all." (From Augustine's Laws published by Viking Press.)

AUGUSTINE'S VIEWS

We are entering a new era as far as defense is concerned. For many years the Department of Defense (DoD) was able, more or less, to provide its own technology and was relatively self-sufficient. Things have changed. Standing out as a new dimension is the increasing importance of optics and electronics, making up 35 percent of the defense budget, and growing. Technology is not being driven in that area by the military and NASA but by the commercial and consumer marketplace where, as a nation, we are not competing well. This places us in a very unusual predicament where our ability to provide national defense is no longer totally within the province of DoD.

That poses a dilemma that we haven't had to face before where, as one example, DoD is dependent upon the U.S. semiconductor industry but defense is only a niche to that industry. And that's a new experience. The clear answer is that we've got to get to where we can compete commercially, and when we try to calculate how we can afford an increase in the DoD budget, by far the best way is to improve the US economy so that the tax base automatically goes up. From that you take the usual one-fourth fraction for defense and get a lot more than by merely squeezing the existing pie. In addition, the ability of the general economy to grow is increasingly important as a source of technology that goes into national defense.

CONSUMER ELECTRONICS

The leading edge technologies in manufacturing are in the consumer market. Furthermore, the engine that drives the high-tech machine, particularly the source of the money for research on the next generation, comes from consumer products. In my judgement, if we cannot compete in the large consumer markets, we will not be able to afford the research it takes to feed into smaller marketplaces such as defense. Companies can always retrench and accept being a niche industry in niche markets. That might be fine for one or two companies in Silicon Valley,

4

but for the whole nation to hide in a niche market will be very tough.

R&D AT THE CROSSROADS

We still do very well in research in this country. Seventeen of the last 24 Nobel prize winners in physics, chemistry and medicine were Americans or individuals involved in research in America. And while we have traditionally been very good as a nation applying that research, we are losing our pre-eminent position. Last year the U.S. Patent Office gave out 14,000 patents to Japanese and 38,000 to U.S. citizens. So we are in good shape in research, slipping in innovation but in terms of applications in the marketplace we are doing very poorly. Take the semiconductor industry: a few years ago we made essentially 100 percent of dynamic RAMS (random access memories) in this country. Today, within two decades, we have less than five percent of the world market. Much of the problem in applications is coupled to our neglect of manufacturing, especially higher rate manufacturing, which is treated in this country as a second class citizen, both by our educational institutions and our companies. And we are now paying the price for having done so.

SOLUTIONS

The solutions have a great deal to do with how we as a nation organize ourselves in the future. Our academic institutions, our companies and our government need to work together rather than as adversaries. One of the principal things that distinguishes the U.S. industrial base from the Japanese is that ours is based on an adversarial system and theirs is a collegial system. I think there is an opportunity for our companies to move together and work with our universities and work with our government. Government cannot do it alone and clearly shouldn't. The Government can provide an environment using tax incentives in terms of research support, companies can work together to avoid duplication and be given anti-trust latitude to do that so that, together, we can become a more competitive force. And if there is one thing that helps fight bureaucracy that's the survival instinct and in industry the survival instinct is very strong at this point .

TRADE BARRIERS

To erect barriers is generally not a very healthy thing to do in the long term. Where we are dealing with a short term anomaly for survival, where one of the most important industries in the next

century (semiconductors) is at stake, maybe we have to make some long term sacrifices to get a short term benefit in select areas. Anti-trust liberalization and banning Japanese entry through acquisition is clearly not an ideal circumstance and it is not even certain that that will solve the problem. Establishing consortia such as Sematech may even be a little too late but in my judgement is a large leap in the right direction.

SERVICE ECONOMY

Maybe you can build a nation based on a service economy. I'm skeptical. But I know for a fact that you can't defend a nation and fight a war with a service economy. And since I am particularly interested in both, I have a great deal of concern over the trend in the U.S. towards a service economy. Fifteen years ago, two-thirds of the graduates at one of the nation's most prestigious business schools went into manufacturing and one-third into investment banking. Today about two-thirds of the best and the brightest go into investment banking, at least they did until October 19th. We all must ask, each of us, what are we doing to build new products, to create new jobs, to better serve the consumer and build a better way of life. The heroes are the guys out in the factory where they are building something, creating jobs, producing products the customer wants and adding something of value to the world. That is not to say that finance is unimportant but it's not obvious to me that you can build a nation based on that part of the world of finance that takes companies, cuts them into pieces and glues them together differently. Certainly the Japanese have not tried that.

SHOCK TREATMENT

It usually takes a shock for this nation to get its act together, so to speak. October 19th (day of the stock market crash in 1987) was a a shock. The loss of our nation's market share has been a shock. The balance of trade, the national debt, the deficit, are other shocks. So when you bring all of these things together there is a growing appreciation of the fact that we have got to do something differently. Unfortunately, the solution is not just one easy thing where the president says now everybody go do this. We've fallen into a number of bad habits over the years. We have neglected manufacturing. Our secondary education system leaves an enormous amount to be desired. Some basic repairs to the infrastructure are in order.

One day, October 19 may be looked

back upon as a very bright day in the country's history in that it began to wake us up to what the national debt is doing. There is a growing awareness in the Congress of a need for action. Last year I had the occasion to testify six or seven times on the semiconductor industry and found intense interest, good questions, a strong awareness and a willingness to act. I am fairly confident that if two years ago I had testified on the same subject, I would not have been invited back. There is reason for optimism within the defense subset of all this, in that the pendulum is now starting to swing back towards equilibrium. Within DoD there is a growing awareness of the need to take actions in such areas as micro-management, premature pricing of production options, the selection of appropriate contract types for development work and support for basic research.

The Defense Department gets good grades on many of their recent actions. Some of the things that they have been doing for some years, such as increasing emphasis on competition, have very positive payoff for the taxpayer and there is no reason to do anything other than to instill a little more balance in those areas and continue on that general course. On the other hand, I would give poor grades on the use of fixed price contracts on high risk development work. While I am encouraged by what is happening today in DoD, in Congress there is less reason for encouragement and that is much harder for any one individual to solve. There is a growing awareness within the Congress of the problems; it's just very difficult for a single individual or organization to make corrective changes. If we were to continue on the course we have been on, we would find ourselves in severe difficulties before the end of the century. That might sound like a long way away but when you are already putting together the 1991 budget it's not.

IMPACT OF TAKEOVERS ON HIGH TECHNOLOGY COMPANIES

Dealing with hostile takeovers is very expensive. One can't help but wonder if you added up the total bill that was spent in this country resisting unwanted takeovers, and plowed that money back into research and development, whether the country as a whole wouldn't be better served. The remedy is part ethics and part legislation. Part of any solution is to take the incentives out of moves that are intended strictly to make very short term profits without any value added. But the takeover business is alive and well although there is a growing frustration within the government and parts of industry against the impact of many takeovers. That's not to say that all takeovers are bad. Friendly takeovers and some hostile ones that fix severe management problems can be beneficial but the notion that acquiring corporations, cutting them up, pasting them together and making a lot of money in the short term with no change in sales, not enhancing customer support and usually decreasing employment, does not seem very beneficial to me...or even very ethical.

THE WORK ETHIC

It's hard to fault the American worker or even in some cases the American manager and I might in that regard comment on the American government employee, with whom I worked hand in hand when I was a public servant. That government employee works as hard as anybody else in most cases but is much maligned. In national terms, our problem is not so much how hard we work; the problem is working smarter. We need to make sure that we are working on the pressure points, the priorities that make a difference. We don't want to spend all our time filling out forms or fighting off takeovers but, rather, those of us in management need to spend more time in the factories and in the research lab. Within an individual company, it's relatively easy to identify your priorities and be sure that your attention is going the way your priorities are. Within the nation as a whole and within DoD, it is my opinion that one can't solve all problems through regulation and legislation, Someone once said that if the only tool in your tool kit is a hammer, every problem tends to look like a nail. If the only thing you can do is write regulations and legislation, that tends to be the solution to every problem. Unfortunately, that does not work. I think we need to back off from our attempt to prevent problems through legislation and give greater latitude to our quality people in government to manage.

DEFENSE SPENDING

The classic question is how much is enough. It's like life insurance; if you don't die you probably shouldn't have any life insurance and defense is much that way. My belief is that we don't spend enough. It's not entirely a matter of what we can "afford," although that's important, but a question of what we

and our allies spend compared with our potential adversaries. And the only way I know how to compare that is not in dollars and rubles but in terms of what's produced. Everyone who has studied the order of battle knows that we tend to be very heavily outnumbered in terms of the U.S. versus the Soviet Union and the Warsaw Pact versus NATO. Clearly we are in a precarious situation and the recent Arms Control Agreements, which I personally support, could, if we don't take the proper follow-up steps, merely make the world safe for conventional war and that would be a tragic outcome.

On spending smartly, I think we spend our money better than the Soviets, but do we spend our money perfectly? My answer is that we are not even close to perfect. There are things we can do to improve the efficiency with which we spend and they are incidentally not in the areas of ferreting out hammers, toilet seats, coffee pots or screwdrivers, on which we spend so much time. The need lies in such areas as improving stability in budgets, stability in people, disciplining the requirements process, thorough testing, emphasizing competition, and things such as that. We've been badly diverted for the last few years with the hammer and toilet seat syndrome. If you are going to run an industry with 1.2 million people and guarantee that not one hammer slips through -- and, incidentally, it's important to say that there is another side to the story of even the hammers and the toilet seats -- you could do that but you probably won't get much of what you need either. If we move in that mode, where we fear failure more than we covet success, we will have come to the point where we won't take prudent and proper risks.

I think that the highest level spending problem is one of not properly estimating the availability of funding in the future. When the average development program takes eight years and the average production program 10 to 15, if you think you are going to have a great deal more money 10 years from now, you tend to start more programs than you will be able to afford. You are then faced with the choice of stretching everything and therefore being inefficient or cancelling some programs. In the latter case, you throw away the money you spent up until the time the program was cancelled. Clearly we need a better forecast of what money will be available. Think of it as a little bit more of the turtle and less of the hare in terms of running defense programs. And one also needs a national

strategy that is coupled to the resources available. It makes no sense for a small Third World nation to decide it's going to have a dominant military force when it can't afford it. Similarly, there are constraints on what the United States can afford to do. We need to be very sure that our political policies and our military capabilities and budgetary strengths all match. It's tough to do...and very dangerous not to do.

BUDGETARY TURBULENCE

A lot of changes are coming in the defense establishment. It's going to get smaller because budgets are decreasing. If you speak to each of my counterparts in the industry, each of us believes that our own company is going to continue to grow; I honestly believe that for my own company. But when you ask if the overall budget is going to increase or decrease, we are unanimous in the belief that it's going to decrease. Somewhere there is a big problem to be sorted out. One thing I think we can say, the industry as a whole is going to shrink. We are seeing mergers, acquisitions, and takeovers in the industry at a far greater rate than in the past and I don't mean the last three months, but over a 20-year trend. The industry is contracting in the sense of companies combining together. You also see a number of companies reporting losses on specific fixed price projects: seven reported $100 million or more losses in the last 18 months. Some of the systems we sold are beginning to come home to haunt our industry . We are in a state of great transition and I suspect that the industry 10 years from now won't look much like today.

THE INDUSTRY HAS NOT FAILED THE COUNTRY

Item for item, most of our military equipment is still pretty much the envy of the world. Most of the world's free nations prefer American or, at least, Western equipment, not necessarily for political reasons but because they believe it's better. The problem we have is that we have to work so hard in our research labs to get three, four years ahead of the Russians -- yet in our management process it's very easy to throw away three or four years. I think that the leverage is perhaps in our ability to manage as much as it is to create new research items. IDI

SHIP AIR DEFENSE

by Philip Farris

Melding old technology with the new, the U.S. Navy utilizes two distinct surface-to-air weapons systems -- the SEASPARROW and the PHALANX.

The NATO SEASPARROW system, a surface launch variant of the air launch SPARROW III, is presently operational on about 50 ships of the seven NATO navies. Utilizing a radar homing guidance system, with target illumination provided by the shipboard MK-91 system radar director, the SEASPARROW is a second generation of the Basic Point Defense Surface Missile System. The missile is 12 feet in length, 8 inches in diameter, with a 40-inch wing span. Weighing 450 pounds, its warhead is of the high explosive, continuous rod type.

Also shown is the PHALANX, the U.S. Navy's first all-weather automatic controlled gun system designed to provide defense against close-in sea-skimming cruise missiles that penetrate outer defense systems. PHALANX is self-contained and readily installed on any ship from patrol boat to aircraft carrier. The complete system weighs 11,350 pounds. Its gun, the M61A1 Vulcan, is electrically controlled, hydraulically driven and provides a rate of fire of 3,000 rounds per minute. Ammunition is 20mm with high density penetrating projectiles. The system became operational in the Navy with its installation onboard the USS ENTERPRISE in mid-1980.

ANTISHIP CRUISE MISSILES

By John Guthrie

The potential military battlefield is now a continuum, extending from below the sea, up through the vapor-laden layers of the atmosphere and into the molecular void of near-earth space: the "High ground" from which all other parts can be observed.

Cruising just above the ocean waves -- perhaps launched just seconds before from a submerged sub -- the modern sea-skimming antiship missile (ASM) is without question one of the deadliest and most probable threats which today face naval surface combatants of all sizes -- from shore patrol boats right on up to blue water guided missile cruisers and carriers. The latest versions of these radar-guided, standoff missiles can approach a ship at an altitude so low that they are below the vessel's radar horizon, lost in the random radar clutter of the sea itself. These missiles can individually, or in salvo, hit and sink a targeted ship, even if it is within a tight formation with other vessels. The coming generations of ASMs will possess even greater flight speed, range, warhead lethality, target discrimination capability and electronic counter-countermeasure (ECCM) capabilities.

Computerized "artificial intelligence" will increase the capability and complexity of onboard cruise missile electronics. These technical improvements -- in missile guidance/navigation accuracy, and in target detection, identification and tracking -- will make all future cruise and glide weapons even more dangerous to ships. Tomorrow's winged "robot weapon" will have pinpoint accuracy and will be able to lock onto any ship, even those employing sophisticated electronic and other countermeasures like chaff, radar-absorbing material (RAM) paints and materials like Plessey, U.K.'s Adran plastic sheeting.

Ships of the future will likely have to defend themselves against subsonic and supersonic cruise missiles which will incorporate advanced "Stealth" and other "low observable" features like covert laser radar and passive, multi-spectral sensors with target recognition. Future cruise weapons may themselves serve as submunition carriers, ejecting high-speed penetrators with high-energy chemical explosives. In addition, ships may be attacked with hypersonic glide vehicles (HGVs) launched from aerospace vehicles or boosted by missile. Like virtually all other winged "flying ro-

bots" of the 21st century, HGVs will navigate by active/passive sensors, with data supplied by the orbiting constellation of global positioning system (GPS) satellites. Flying towards its target at Mach 10 or 12, an HGV will be capable of performing kinetic-energy attacks that punch through a ship from top-to-bottom. Such a maneuvering HGV attacker could not be repelled by even today's terminal defense missiles or high rate-of-fire, close-in-weapon-systems (CIWS), like the British Goalkeeper and American Phalanx.

The operational baseline technology for these various classes of deadly, winged cruise weapons of tomorrow can be seen in the operational versions of very lethal sea-skimming missiles currently on active duty around the world. With varying degrees of sophistication, these weapons are currently manufactured by nations as diverse as China, Britain, France, Italy, the United States and the USSR. The requisite technology base for sea skimmers is well within the grasp of a host of smaller nations which have their own aerospace infrastructure; and one can easily expect many of them to develop missiles for use in regional naval conflicts.

(Left) The Aerospatiale EXOCET MM40 is test fired
from aboard ship. The MM40 is the surface-to-surface
version of the EXOCET.
(Above) Damage to commercial vessel resulting
from a direct hit of an EXOCET missile.

The requirement of the U.S. Navy to be capable of conducting global military operations against the entire spectrum of potentially hostile naval forces has led to the creation of the HARPOON antiship weapon system. The HARPOON is manufactured by McDonnell Douglas Astronautics Company and can be launched from surface ships, aircraft, submarines, and shore-based installations. With a standoff range of over 50 nautical miles, the HARPOON allows over-the-horizon targeting and provides the U.S. and many of its allies with a new dimension in accuracy, firepower, and launch platform safety, as well as survivabilty.

Depending on the choice of launch platform, the HARPOON Weapon System consists of the missile and the HARPOON shipboard/aircraft/encapsulated (submarine) command and launch subsystem; a (buoyant) capsule subsystem and support subsystem which permits the HARPOON to be handled logistically as a "round of ammunition." Following initial checkout at a Naval Weapons Station (NWS), each HARPOON is deployed. After a three-year duty cycle, each HARPOON returns to the NWS for a series of ALL-UP-ROUND maintenance tests. While deployed with operating units, the HARPOON's guidance, warhead, sustainer engine, control and booster sections/subsystems can be monitored with a built-in-test (BIT).

Today, the HARPOON can be found on over 200 U.S. surface ships and attack subs. Deployment candidates include PHM patrol hydrofoils, FF-1052 class frigates, FFG-7 guided missile frigates, DD and DDG class destroyers, CG and CGN class guided missile cruisers, BB battleships; and classes 594, 637, 688 and nuclear attack submarines. U.S. Naval aircraft capable of launching the HARPOON include the P-3 and S-3 antisubmarine warfare patrol; A-6, A-7E and F/A-18 attack; and U.S. Air Force B-52.

The 13.5-inch diameter HARPOON missile can be launched from standard torpedo launch tubes. It can also be fired from missile launchers designed for the ASROC antisub rocket, and for the TARTAR surface-to-air missile. For launching from ships and submarines, HARPOON employs a 12,000-pound-thrust rocket booster to accelerate the missile for 2.9 seconds to cruising velocity. Following a (sub) surface launch, booster separation occurs at roughly 1,300 feet. At that point, the HARPOON's 98-pound, single-spool turbojet sustainer engine kicks in with 600 pounds thrust, burning 100 pounds JP-4 fuel at 41,000 rpm. In the future, a denser fuel, JP-10, will increase the HARPOON's range to nearly 60 miles. Attitude control of the missile following jet engine startup is affected by the guidance system; and the missile descends until the pull out command is given by the guidance section's short-pulse radar altimeter. The HARPOON then cruises just above the wave tops to its target at a speed of Mach .85.

The HARPOON can be targeted with data from aircraft radar, sonar, ESM, "third party" and periscope inputs. Various launch modes and seeder search patterns enhance the missile's probability of hitting a designated target. The missile's 488.5-pound high explosive warhead is contained in an armor-penetrating casing. A pressure probe and contact fuse with delay circuit ensures that warhead detonation occurs within the target's hull, enhancing the likelihood of secondary explosions and fire propagation in spite of modern advances in ship design and damage control measures.

Thirteen years after HARPOON production began, over 4,900 missiles have been ordered by the U.S. Navy and by some 17 foreign countries including NATO allies -- Saudi Arabia, Egypt, Israel, Australia, Japan, South Korea, Thailand and Pakistan. The falling value of the U. S. dollar makes the HARPOON an attractively sophisticated weapon system to foreign customers. Competing with the U.S. HARPOON for export sales are virtually all the other cruise missile manufacturers in the world.

The French EXOCET, in its various configurations for aircraft and (sub) surface-launch (AM39 air-to-surface; MM38 and MM40 surface-to-surface; SM39 subsurface) is probably the best known of the current generation of sea-skimming ASMs. Since the missile entered operational service in 1972, some 3,000 rounds have been manufactured for the French military and for the air forces and navies of 27 other countries. The missile gained notoriety in May 1987 for its use by the Iraqi Air Force against the U.S. Navy frigate, USS STARK, in the Persian Gulf.

Built by the Tactical Missiles Division of Aerospatiale, the EXOCET family has evolved into the current family of four missile configurations to permit a wide choice of basing/launch configurations. All versions fly on cruciform wings with solid rocket boost and sustainer engines at about Mach 0.93; their range varies from 40-70 km, depending on missile type and firing conditions. The ship-launched MM38 has a maximum range of 42 km. Weighing 1,750 kilograms (kg), the MM38 can be launched from standard and light-weight firing units, permitting smaller patrol craft to be armed with the system. The MM38 guidance is inertial during the weapon's approach phase, with active homing during the terminal phase.

The 1,892-pound MM40 is the big brother of the MM38; and has an over-the-horizon range of 70 km. Like the SEA SKUA, the MM40 can lock onto its target with the radar illumination of a scout helicopter, in order to identify a single ship in a group to be hit. The MM40 uses the same propulsion system as the air-launched AM39 version. Besides offering the same wide variety of ship-basing options as the lighter MM38, the MM40 is also available in a truck-mounted or fixed-sited shore battery version.

The air-launched, AM39 version of the EXOCET offers a 50-70-km range, fire-and-forget capability to jet fighters, maritime patrol aircraft and helicopter launch platforms. The 1,441-pound AM39 first entered service in 1978. The sub-launched version of the missile, the SM39, can be fired from torpedo tubes; its targeting makes few depth, bearing or speed requirements on the launch sub. Launched in a watertight, powered and guided underwater vehicle called a VSM, the SM39 separates from the VSM at low altitude after breaking the surface some distance from the sub. EXOCET warhead weight is reportedly around 360 pounds.

Clockwise from left:

AEROSPATIALE
Supersonic Antiship Missile;
EXOCET AM 39 / SUPER PUMA;
EXOCET AM 39 / MIRAGE 2000;
Artist view of the under water
launching of an EXOCET SM 39.

The 1,320-pound SEA EAGLE is British Aerospace's entry in the international market for long-range ASM. Like most other ASMs, the body of the four-meter long SEA EAGLE contains five sections: guidance, control, warhead, fuel and propulsion. Like the HARPOON, the SEA EAGLE utilizes four cruciform wings with four control surfaces in line with the wings. The missile flies at Mach .90 under the power of a Microturbo TRI-60 turbojet.

Before being launched from an aircraft like the Sea Harrier, Buccaneer, Hawk or Sea King helicopter, the SEA EAGLE is programmed by the flight crew with target positioning and attack profile data. The flight crew can also program the missile with target selection criteria when grouped targets are encountered. Missile launch can take place at low and high altitudes, with the missile descending to sea-skimming height following turbojet startup. Flying along the programmed flight path to its target, the SEA EAGLE's active radar seeker can illuminate the designated ship from a distance of 30 kilometers.

This high power seeker permits the missile to lock onto the target outside the range of the target ship's own defensive ECM capability. Even when exposed to jamming ECM, the SEA EAGLE's seeker can "burn through" and obtain lock-on. The SEA EAGLE uses a computer-controlled ECCM suite to maintain radar lock even as the missile enters the ship's optimal ECM envelope. During its terminal flight, the missile flies even closer to the deck, so as to enter the target as close to the waterline as possible. Although warhead size is classi-

Sea Eagle Long Range Antiship Missile on a Royal Air Force Hawk T-1

fied, it's thought to be about the same as the HARPOON.

The British Aerospace SEA SKUA is the smaller cousin of the SEA EAGLE. It is the U.K.'s primary, helicopter-launched, air-to-surface weapon; and can also be carried by fixed-wing air-craft. Just 2.5 meters in length and 319 pounds in weight, the SKUA uses solid rocket booster and sustainer engines for flight. Because of their small volume and weight, up to four SEA SKUAs can be carried by shipborne or shore-based helicopters for ripple-firing against well-

defended targets or for coordinated attacks with two or more helicopters. British ships can remain undetected as they attack hostile vessels armed with long-range ship-to-ship missiles.

When a patrol helicopter detects, identi-fies and tracks a potential target, the flight crew will close to within 15 km at low level and then climb rapidly to missile re-lease height. The helicopter's own radar illuminates the target ship and the mis-sile's homing head locks onto the reflect-ed radar signal. After release, the missile drops away from the helicopter before the

solid booster ignites. During boost, the SKUA descends to an intermediate, sea-skimming height as its azimuth and height guidance loops close. As the missile ap-proaches its target, it descends to the terminal skimming height, pre-selected by the flight crew for the size and type of tar-get being attacked. Throughout the at-tack, the target remains illuminated by the radar of the launch helicopter, which maintains a safe distance from the termi-nal defense zone of the target ship.

SEA SKUA warhead detonation occurs after penetrating the target's hull.

Another European cruise missile, the Franco-Italian OTOMAT, will soon offer a submarine torpedo-launch option. The Milas version of OTOMAT is expected to enter service with the French Navy in 1992. The Milas will carry advanced, antisubmarine torpedoes (French Murene or Italian Whitehead A290) to a distance of some 30 nautical miles (nm) from the launching sub.

The OTOMAT is the joint venture of Matra S.A. of France and the Italian firm of Oto Melara. At approximately 700 kg each missile and launcher weight (1,400 kg total), the OTOMAT is the heavyweight of Western cruise missiles. It has an effective range of 60 km and is boosted into flight with a pair of strap-on Hotchkiss-Brandt/SNP1 solid rockets. At Mach 0.9 flight speed, the solid boosters are jettisoned and the OTOMAT cruises on the power of a 900-pound-thrust Turbomeca Arbizon turbojet. Advances in the guidance of both French and Italian versions of the missile permit a single weapon to receive midcourse updates. The Italian TESEO guidance set can receive updates from aircraft. The French ERATO set can only be updated from the launch platform. Both of these updated versions of the OTOMAT are referred to as Mk 1. A compact Mk 2 version has been developed to permit the doubling of missile launchers in the same amount of deck space as the Mk 1.

The Soviet Union, reportedly, utilizes the same kind of midcourse update system as the French ERATO system in its advanced ASMs. The Soviets pioneered the development of ASMs in the early 1960s, and they have been continuously upgrading their operational systems -- and introducing new ones -- ever since. The design of Soviet cruise missiles emphasizes the high speed and large warheads (many systems are nuclear-capable). Therefore, many potential ASMs have dual-capability in theater warfare. Many Soviet cruise missiles are supersonic, with flight speeds as high as Mach 3.5 and can carry conventional warheads weighing as much as 2,200 pounds. Soviet sea skimmers like the solid rocket-powered SS-N-7 (NATO code-named Siren) operate at Mach 0.95 with a range of 30-35 nm. It carries a 1,100-pound warhead. The SS-N-21 has a range of about 1,600 nm and is nuclear-capable.

All of these ASMs confront navies of the world with ominous threats of unprecedented measure. Others to come will present surface ships even greater challenges for survival. IDI

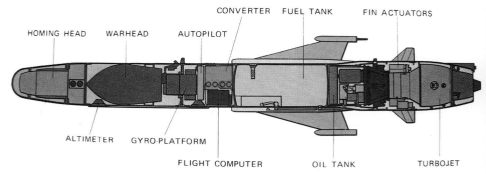

The OTOMAT antiship missile system is suitable for installation in ships of varying tonnage--from patrol craft to frigates (as shown left). Its high explosive warhead is capable of penetrating armor 90mm thick at a 90 degree angle of impact.

2	Helicopter carriers
4	Destroyers
32	Frigates
13	Corvettes
25	Fast Patrol Boats
7	Hydrofoils

83 Ships:

OTOMAT Missile System is installed, or scheduled for installation on board of 83 ships of Italian and foreign Navies.

BOOSTERS

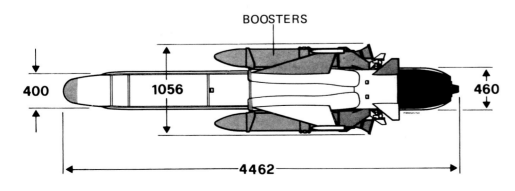

400   1056   460
4462

"SAW SUB---SANK SAME"
An Historical Look at the USS ENGLAND--Sub Hunter Extraordinaire

by
Tari Schnepf-Lightbody

The 1944 Pacific sun blistered over an eerily calm sea as the destroyer escort (DE) ENGLAND roiled the vacant expanse of ocean between the coast of New Guinea and the Japanese fortress of Truk in the Marianas. On routine patrol with the DEs GEORGE and RABY, the ENGLAND's crew, fresh from stateside, found the war slightly less than exciting. Stirred by American victories in the Solomon's, trained as subhunters, they found their sharply honed combat readiness dulled by the endless routine of escort and patrol duties.

On the ENGLAND's open bridge, Executive Officer John Williamson stared endlessly at the empty sea and bemoaned the lack of entries in the ship's battle-log. As he conned the ship in idle frustration, he wasn't aware that in the radio room the ENGLAND's skipper, Lieutenant Commander Walton 'Walt' Pendleton watched the communications officer decode a message from Admiral Halsey's headquarters that was to make the ENGLAND the most famous DE in history, and alter the course of the Pacific War!

The bridge speaker erupted in a crackling bark, "Johnny, come down to the CIC we've got a hot flash from COMCORT!"

Lieutenant Williamson turned over the ship's CON to the OOD and hurried down the ladder that led to the ENGLAND's combat nerve center. There, in a small, hot and sweaty compartment, skipper Pendleton, a thickset, stern faced man, looked over the green glow of the lighted plotting table.

"Third fleet flagship reports a PBY plane spotted a Japanese sub in our patrol area. They pulled the plug before the PBY could make a run, but they've ordered us to intercept."

Williamson knew that since Bougainville had been cut off and bypassed that the Japanese were using subs as supply ships to service their isolated garrisons. Knowing the sub's position when spotted by the Navy plane, and its likely destination, Commander Pendleton plotted a course to let them intercept the sub a day's sailing away.

At flank speed, they altered course northeast of Bougainville and bid farewell to the jeep carrier HOGGART BAY which they had been escorting. Together with DEs GEORGE and RABY, the ENGLAND's bow cut a sharp swath through the gentle Pacific swells. Paced 4,000 yards apart, the three ships steamed in an oblique line making sonar sweeps that would, hopefully, detect the Japanese submarine.

Eagerly, Lieutenant Williamson made the first entry into the battle-log of the USS ENGLAND. No sooner had he completed his task when Pendleton reported that the sonar had just picked up a definite echo!

Yet, Williamson couldn't believe they had made contact so soon. They were still several miles east of the expected intercept point and a full day ahead of schedule. Knowing the submarine's top underwater speed was nine knots, Williamson arrived at the only conclusion he could -- there were two submarines.

Pendleton had come to the same opinion, and before he could nod in agreement Williamson had depressed the signal switch that sounded General Quarters.

Men flew out from every hatch. In moments, the ENGLAND had every battle station manned. Walt Pendleton returned to the bridge while Williamson remained in CIC control to coordinate sonar bearings to the bridge.

As the ship charged into the attack, her sister DEs, RABY and GEORGE, gave her a wide berth. Once the CIC reported they were within range of the unknown target, Pendleton gave the order to fire the Hedgehog rockets. Hedgehog projectiles would explode only on contact with an object. If nothing was hit, they sank unobtrusively to the ocean's floor.

With a blast that numbed the forward gun crew's ears, 24 rocket projectiles blasted into the air over their heads, shot in a wide arc forward of the bow.

Wasting no time, the skipper ordered another full salvo, then another and another. Somewhere under the deep and silent sea an explosion sounded. The Echo-ranger pantograph swung in frantic sweeps across the graph paper, literally going off its track in response to the unseen blast. Off the port quarter a lookout spotted a cluster of bubbles rising out of a turbulent patch of sea. Pendleton gave the order for hard to port and ordered another Hedgehog salvo.

This fifth attack proved the virtues of Pendleton's tenacity. Ten seconds after the fifth salvo hit the water, the fathometer reported several muffled blasts at 54 fathoms. Stopped over their quarry, they little expected the shuddering blast that let go deep under the ship's keel. Every man aboard was knocked off his feet. Cups jumped from the galley's stowage racks. The blast was so violent that some of the antenna rigging snapped. At first, the crew thought they had been torpedoed. But, as Commander Pendleton staggered to his feet, he realized their elusive prize had blown up directly beneath them.

Later that evening, Pendleton and Williamson relaxed in the wardroom with the second escort division commander, C.A. Thorwall. Though pleased with the day's events, they still could not understand how they had come upon the sub so quickly. Arguing tactics, Pendleton maintained that the sub sighted originally had not yet arrived. He wanted to continue towards Truk, rationalizing that in another day they would intercept the cargo-sub. Commander Thorwall was concerned over the HOGGART BAY being unescorted by her DEs. Afraid their little entourage would be outmatched if it ran headlong into the Japanese fleet, he felt the three DEs should call off the hunt.

The debate was quickly settled early on the morning of May 21. A coded message from Halsey's flagship reported that a patrol plane had spotted another Japanese sub north of the ENGLAND's position. Halsey had deduced from these concurrent sightings that the enemy had strung a line of submersible scouts west from Truk to keep an eye on the Task Force groups. Since the ENGLAND and her companions were in the vicinity of the latest sighting, they were ordered to investigate.

The following morning the GEORGE made radar contact with a surfaced Japanese submarine, range 14,000 yards. All three DEs bored in for the kill, but by the time they got within gunnery range, the sub had dived. The GEORGE's searchlight scanned the black waters. But it was from the ENGLAND's bridge that the ghostly shadow of the submarine was spotted.

Two Hedgehog volleys later, the thunder of another underwater explosion was felt all over the ship. An oilslick proved the submarine's demise and floating debris confirmed that its end had been swift. Two subs in three days was not a record, but it was something special for the neophyte sailors to write home about.

Unfortunately, they had little time for letterwriting, as less than 24 hours after the ship's second victory, the trio of destroyer escorts made contact again.

The RABY's skipper, Commander R. Scott, signalled that he had a strong 'pip' on his radar screen. After receiving the message, a sleepy-eyed Walt Pendleton appeared in the CIC wearing a steel helmet, sandals and a bathrobe. Seeing that the ENGLAND lay off the RABY's port track and that the GEORGE lay off the starboard, Pendleton knew the submarine had to come within range of one or the other.

Soon after the sub dove for the ocean floor, the RABY cut loose with a virtually continuous salvo of Hedgehogs. Then, almost exhausting her ammo, the ship retired and let the GEORGE continue.

Evaluating the situation, Williamson came up with an idea which Pendleton adopted. When the GEORGE signalled that she had lost contact with the prey, Pendleton allowed a full 15 minutes to pass, lulling the submarine into believing the chase was off. After ordering an 'S' turn, Pendleton listened to the sonar and heard it boom with a signal and definite fix.

Low on Hedgehog ammunition, they fired only 12 rockets, and waited. Minutes later, an undeniable roar echoed below. The ENGLAND had scored another victory!

It did not take long for word to spread along other ships that the DE was single-handedly wiping out the Japanese submarine fleet. Her record victories brought cries of a demand for confirmation from Fleet Headquarters which felt cheated and overshadowed by the tiny ship.

American authorities were not the only ones concerned over the ENGLAND's exploits. In far off Truk, Japanese Admiral Toyoda paused to examine the rapid disappearance of three of his stalwart scouting submarines: the 1-16, the RO-106, and the RO-104.

The USS ENGLAND, unwittingly, not only cut his scout force in half, but she also gave the baffled Japanese Admiral the impression that a huge task force was charging towards Palau and obliterating his scouts one by one. From his faulty intelligence, he began ordering planes from Guam to the Pelews to bolster their sagging defenses.

If Admiral Toyoda had any doubts about the huge American task force rip-

ping towards him, they were dispelled when word reached him that another of his subs, the RO-116, had mysteriously stopped sending a station report in mid-sentence.

The RO-116 met its demise at the expert hands of Walt Pendleton on the morning of May 24th. The only serious problem confronting the trio of DEs was that they were now dangerously low on fuel, stores and, most importantly, depth charges and Hedgehog ammunition. Commander Thorwall at last had his way when the trio reversed course and started back towards Manus.

Cruising over the same course they had followed when going north, Pendleton let the crew go to semi-combat readiness with only half the guns and battle stations manned. Men off watch dropped where they stood rather than go below to the sweltering compartments. Curling up over, under, and on gun mounts, ventilators, liferafts, torpedo tubes, hatches, and one another, the exhausted seamen longed for a few uninterrupted hours of rest. Even the ever-present, ever-ready Walt Pendleton disappeared below to his state room, leaving the OOD on the bridge.

An hour before midnight the Japanese submarine RO-108 spotted the thin trails of smoke of three ships approaching from the southeast. To 75 fathoms the sub dove, listening as the whir of propellers droned overhead. There were depth charges yet the Japanese soundman cringed at the ship noises so close above. Why didn't they attack?

The answer came in a thunderous blast. Four simultaneous explosions peppered RO-108's hull, ripping open the forward torpedo room, battery compartment and control room.

The ENGLAND had done it again. Not a Hedgehog was left aboard any of the three DEs, but Pendleton's unerring tactics had obliterated their fifth sub with only one salvo of 12 Hedgehog projectiles.

By the time the ENGLAND returned to Seeadler Harbor on Manus, a reception committee awaited that did not meet its equal until the entire fleet sailed into Tokyo Harbor two years later. Ship after ship saluted the ENGLAND with all ensigns flying from the halyards and thousands of white uniformed sailors standing at attention. Though the RABY and GEORGE shared no small part in the feat, it was clearly the ENGLAND's day.

The crew's brief but entertaining liberty celebration ashore was not to last long. While her crew scouted the bars and canteens, the destroyer SPANGLER, sent from Tulagi with a fresh supply of ammuni-

tion, busily replenished the ENGLAND for yet another patrol sweep.

The following morning, May 28th, the ENGLAND set sail in company with RABY, GEORGE, and SPANGLER to rendezvous off Manus with the HOGGART BAY and the destroyers HAZELWOOD and McCORD.

Only two days elapsed before Pendleton proved his expertise again. In a four-hour attack on yet another submarine, the destroyers HAZELWOOD and SPANGLER, and the DEs GEORGE and RABY, failed to touch the enemy. Picking up the sonar 'pip', Pendleton sailed into the arena slowly and added one salvo of Hedgehogs to the torrent of rockets hurled by the other destroyers.

All salvos missed and a sudden message from the bridge informed Pendleton that Admiral Halsey's flagship had ordered an immediate withdrawal from the attack. They were too close to Truk's aircraft.

"Withdraw hell!" Pendleton shouted. Grabbing the mike, he literally shamed the commander of Escort Division 40 to let them continue their hunt.

A shout of joy echoed from the DE as her engineers poured on flank speed and sent her bow churning into the silent waves that hid her prey.

Using every trick in the book, Pendleton soon had a firm sonar fix and ordered a full Hedgehog salvo. Twenty-four rockets cascaded into the water, disappearing in a swirl of foam. Twenty seconds later, a soul-tearing crash smashed the ENGLAND's hull as deep underwater explosions signalled the swift finish of their sixth submarine.

Performing a feat unparalleled in history, the USS ENGLAND was awarded the Presidential Unit Citation by President Roosevelt. In 12 days, she not only sank the enemy submarines 1-16, RO-106, RO-104, RO-116, RO-108, and RO-105, but also managed to give Admiral Toyoda the impression that a major American fleet was driving to attack Palau. Nothing could have been further from the truth. For in reality, the attack was headed for the Marianas. Unknowingly, the ENGLAND threw the Japanese off and left them severely handicapped in repulsing the Marianas attack.

Walt Pendleton's terse combat report, "Sighted Sub, Sank Same," was memorialized in the annals of Naval warfare. As a tribute to his ship's feats, the Chief of Naval Operations, Admiral E. J. King, pledged, "There will always be an ENGLAND in the United States Navy!" This pledge was fulfilled on October 6,1960, when DLG-22 was assigned the name USS ENGLAND. ᴅ

U.S. MINE SWEEPERS

DISTANT DUTY FOR WOODEN SHIPS
by Philip Farris

U.S. minesweepers in the Persian Gulf have had an indispensable role to carry out. Keeping the waterways clear of mines for the safe passage of American and allied ships is an all-consuming task -- requiring expert personnel and formidable ships. This important mission has been performed ever so capably by such minesweepers as the USS ENHANCE and INFLICT (shown in accompanying photos).

Sea-mines are effective and psychologically powerful weapons. In the Persian Gulf, they have menaced the ships of all nations in the area -- until U.S. minesweepers arrived on the scene. An example of their importance is the achievement of the USS INFLICT which, in her first seven days scanning the Farsi minefield, found 10 mines. This kind of success enables other U.S. ships and the tankers they are protecting to pass safely through Persian Gulf waterways. ᴵᴰᴵ

MINE COUNTERMEASURES:

A EUROPEAN PERSPECTIVE

by Tony Velocci

Soviet military planners have long searched for ways to ensure victory in combat against the North Atlantic Treaty Organization (NATO). Yet, despite the great volume of writing in the West about the Soviet military, comparatively little attention has focused on what may be its most effective weapon at the outset of any conventional war: the ability to mine the waters in and around West European Ports.

The strategy (minnozagraditel 'nyye deystviya), well documented, would employ extensive mine barriers (minnyye zagrazhdyeniya) to cut off the resupply of reinforcements and materiel, 90 percent of which would be transported by ships sailing from the U.S. That resupply would be crucial to NATO's ability to repel a Warsaw Pact invasion. Outgunned and outnumbered, Western armies would be hard pressed to sustain a strong defense for more than several weeks before shortages impaired their ability to fight.

Within NATO, primary responsibility for countering the Soviet mine warfare threat rests with European navies, which have a collective mine countermeasures (MCM) force of about 225 or so vessels. Their task would be to keep major ports, like Antwerp, and their approaches clear of deadly mines that could prevent U.S. cargo ships from reaching their destination and impair the movement of NATO submarines.

While the Europeans' mine countermeasures muscle may seem more than adequate for the job, especially compared with U.S. MCM resources -- 28 MCM vessels and 23 helicopters -- the Allied navies would face a daunting task.

The Europeans' MCM vessels -- there are no helicopters assigned to mine warfare -- are not autonomous blue water forces that can be quickly deployed from one area to another. Rather, they must be considered in the context of campaign regions and against the threat posed against them in those areas. "Taking these factors into account, the picture is worse than might be believed on first examination of the statistics alone," says Admiral Sir William Staveley, Chief of Naval Staff in Great Britain and NATO's former Commander-in-Chief, Eastern Atlantic. He also points out that "despite our qualitative im-

provements in recent years, we are short on numbers if the threat posed against us is widespread."

That would seem to be a strong possibility. The Soviet Union has the world's largest stockpile of mines, perhaps 250,000 or more, as well as an extensive capability to lay mines from all types of surface ships, submarines and aircraft.

Soviet merchant ships are also equipped for discrete minelaying. On a daily basis, more than 70 Soviet and East European-flag merchant vessels are in North and West European ports, and they could be expected to covertly mine NATO port approaches before the outbreak of any war. In fact, time delay actuation would permit such operations months before the first shot was ever fired.

Warsaw Pact submarines would have the primary role in creating minefields whose widespread distribution would probably stretch NATO's MCM resources. The approaches to ports, bases, straits and interior waterways would be mined simultaneously. Specific targets would likely include the area around Faroes/Shetlands/Norway to hamper reinforcements of NATO's northern flank, the Greenland-Iceland-United Kingdom Gap, and the southeast approaches to the United Kingdom, as well as virtually the entire English Channel.

"Europe could have double the MCM resources now available to it and still have its hands full combatting Soviet mines," according to a Pentagon naval analyst.

For years, NATO's European navies paid relatively little attention to the mine warfare threat. The prevailing view was that merchant shipping could be best protected by concentrating resources on strengthening antisurface, antisubmarine, and antiaircraft defenses. Then, in the 1970s a more sobering assessment of the mine warfare threat emerged, and extensive shipbuilding programs for MCM vessels were launched by several NATO countries.

Since that time, minehunting has become the most effective form of defensive active mine countermeasures within the Western Alliance. Minehunters are complex ships with sophisticated sensors, navigation gear and ship maneuvering systems. There is a high level of commonality among the Western navies and, for their size, the ships are expensive compared with their predecessors. As a result, Western Europe has been able to procure fewer MCM vessels. On the positive side, the newer minehunters/sweepers are far more effective, with the ability to detect and destroy most types of mines now in the Soviet inventory, including those using complex firing circuits and sophisticated shipcounters. They also have more advanced self-defensive features, such as antimagnetic hulls and engines to minimize their own vulnerability.

There are about 170 minesweepers and 90 minehunters among NATO's European navies. Some of these have the dual capability to hunt and sweep for mines. Many of these vessels are nearing the end of their useful life, although a substantial number are to be replaced with modern MCM craft over the next five to 12 years. Belgium, the Federal German Republic (West Germany), Italy, Sweden, the United Kingdom (UK), and Spain all have major construction programs underway. West Germany alone expects to add 20 new MCM vessels to its fleet by 1996. Sweden will commission six new vessels this year.

Many of these vessels will deploy variable depth sonars and remotely-controlled submersible mine neutralization systems that will significantly enhance their performance in deep waters. In shallower waters, NATO's European navies can be "moderately optimistic" about their MCM capabilities to counter the mine threat, according to Admiral Staveley.

The British Hunt class minehunters/sweepers are among the most capable and sophisticated MCM craft to join the NATO inventory. The Royal Navy has 12 of these and is scheduled to commission another one during early 1988.

The 615-ton, 187-foot vessels combine magnetic sweep gear with two PAP 104 remotely controlled submersibles, a Sperry towed acoustic generator and conventional Oropsea sweeps. GRP hulls minimize the ship's magnetic signature. They are powered by twin Ruston-Paxman 3,800-horsepower diesels capable of speeds of 16 knots. A hydraulic drive permits slow running up to eight knots.

The Royal Navy's Hunt class minehunters/sweepers help provide the UK with the largest MCM force among its European counterparts, with a total of 24 minehunters, 12 fleet minesweepers and five coastal minesweepers.

West Germany has the second largest mine countermeasures fleet, with a total of 37 vessels, according to **Jane's Fighting Ships**. These include 12 minehunters, 27 coastal minesweepers and 18 inshore minesweepers. All of West Germany's sweepers are wooden hulled vessels, and are fitted mainly with non-magnetic engines to counter the high threat of mines in the shallow West German waters.

Its MCM force will be expanded with the addition of 10 Type 343 fast minesweeping vessels, which will have anti-magnetic hulls. They will be constructed over the next several years. The West German Navy is also planning construction of 20 Type 332 minehunters after the completion of the Type 343 craft. The first 10 are scheduled to join the fleet in the 1992-93 timeframe, with the remainder to be commissioned by 1999. Most of West Germany's MCM vessels currently in service were built in the mid-1950s and 1960s.

Italy has the next largest MCM fleet, consisting of 11 minehunters, four ocean minesweepers and 10 coastal minesweepers. Eight minehunters and eight improved Lerici class minehunting craft are under construction. All machinery aboard the Lerici class vessels (470 tons displacement) currently in service is mounted on vibration dampers and the main engines are made of antimagnetic material. Minehunting equipment includes a precision navigation system with automatic plotting and data processing capability, and one Pluto mine neutralization system.

Italy's FIAR S.P.A. is developing the AN/SQQ-14/IT, an improved version of the AN/SQQ-14 sonar manufactured by General Electric, in response to the Italian Navy's requirements for the Lerici 2a series of MCM craft. They're scheduled to enter service over the next several years. This mine-detecting/classification system was designed primarily for the detection of sea-bottom mines.

It is a two-frequency, variable-depth, beam-steering sonar, and uses a curved face projector, line-array hydrophones and modulation scanning. To meet the operational requirements of modern MCM, a speed scan unit is used in conjunction with the sonar search system for route survey, which issues print-out of the seabed data received. The system enables two operators to simultaneously detect and classify mines.

The Netherlands contributes 24 mine countermeasures vessels to NATO's European MCM force. These include 13 Alkmaar Tripartite minehunters (displacement 510 tons) and 11 coastal minesweepers. Their original requirement for 15 minehunters and minesweepers has been modified because of NATO's need for additional deep water sweepers. The Netherlands is discussing the design of such vessels that could meet the requirements of other NATO navies, such as those of Belgium and Norway. The minehunters are equipped with mechanical sweep gear as well as two remotely operated submersibles.

Belgium's mine countermeasures fleet is comprised of 10 Tripartite minehunters/sweepers (displacement 510 tons) based on a design developed in cooperation with the navies of France and the Netherlands. The hull is fiberglass, and the ships are fully protected against nuclear-biological-chemical contamination. It carries six divers when minehunting. The active MCM equipment includes two PAP 104 remotely operated submersibles for minehunting, and mechanical sweep gear for medium-depth waters.

Belgium is studying the design of a minesweeper as a follow-on to the hunters to cope with bottom mines laid in the southern end of the North Sea; they sink too far into the soft sand to be detected by minehunters.

Other European countries contributing to NATO's MCM force include Norway, with eight coastal minesweeper/hunters; Spain, with four ocean minesweepers and eight coastal minesweepers; Turkey, with 22 coastal minesweepers, four inshore sweepers and seven minehunters; and Greece, with 14 coastal minesweepers.

These MCM vessels would encounter -- one way or the other -- every type of mine in the Soviet arsenal, with the possible exception of nuclear mines. This would include moored or buoyant mines, ground mines and self-propelled, usually homing, mobile mines. Target, water depth and the required laying point would determine which types the Soviets and other Warsaw Pact navies employed.

Moored and ground mines are generally laid in relatively shallow water, although they also can be used in deeper water. They're most effective when fitted with contact or antenna fuzing against nearby targets. Moored mines

on a long tether are vulnerable to simple mechanical sweeping as well as the effects of currents.

Ground mines, in contrast, may not be swept by simple mechanical means and are less likely to drift. Even with their larger warhead they are still restricted to deployment in relatively shallow water. Depending on their warhead size, ground mines are considered the most effective against surface vessels down to a nominal depth of 60 meters.

Mobile mines may be one of two types: tethered or self-propelled. The former is tethered to the seabed by a sinker at water depths of about 250 meters. The

tethered mine has a listening sonar array that, on detection of a target, activates the mine. Once it is launched, the mine is either propelled or rises due to its own buoyancy towards the target ship.

Warsaw Pact navies would use self-propelled mines against heavily defended areas of shallower water, such as the approaches to ports and straits. This type of mine is best exemplified by the submarine-launched variety. After reaching the area to be mined, normally a harbor or inlet, the torpedo sinks to the seabed. It is equipped with the sensors and signal processing apparatus of a conventional ground mine, and will func

tion on the presence of a target at its closest point of approach.

Many, if not all, types of Soviet mines are made available to Eastern European navies of the Warsaw Pact. This inventory includes mines that, in spite of their obsolescence, have been retained in service, in some cases since the end of World War II. Although they are likely to prove highly vulnerable to modern mine countermeasures, they nevertheless could pose an effective threat and would absorb a significant number of NATO's MCM resources.

Clearing a field of moored contact mines, such as those found in Persian

Gulf waters in recent months, can be done with straightforward sweeping. Clearing mines that explode from magnetism, sound or pressure can be more difficult. In fact, there currently are no operational sweeps that can counter mines with pressure components, notes naval expert and Pentagon consultant, Norman Friedman. Mines with arming delays are also unaffected. If the mines are equipped with complex ship counters, this will significantly increase the sweeping effort required as well.

The navies of most European NATO members employ mine-hunting submersibles that search for mines and destroy

them with explosive charges. These submersibles are effective, extend a navy's MCM capabilities and lessen the risk in mine disposal.

Examples of minehunting submersibles used by NATO navies include the Italian MIN, the German Penguin B-3, the Swedish Sea Eagle, the Minnow developed by Britain's Marconi Underwater Systems Ltd., and the U.S. MNS.

In 1986, for example, the Royal Navy selected the Mark V, the most advanced version of the 104, for its new Hunt class vessels. Its advantage over other systems is its unique ability to destroy mines in water up to 300 meters deep and at a standoff distance of 600 meters. It's also the only MNS capable of carrying a 100-kg explosive charge. It operates on batteries, with cable dispensed from the MNS vehicle. The Mark V is employed by French-Belgian-Netherlands Tripartite minehunters as well.

The MNS vehicle measures three meters in length, 1.3 meters wide, 1.3 meters in height, and weighs some 600 kg. It has a maximum speed of six knots. Although the basic design was conceived over 10 years ago, specifically to counter ground or moored mines, it is still considered highly effective.

The Mark V is the third generation PAP 104. It incorporates various advanced features, including: a fiber optic cable linking it to the mother ship that helps to reduce drag while increasing digital transmission of data; and both a TV camera and an identification nearfield sonar. It also has the capability of carrying a disposal charge and two cutters simultaneously.

When a minehunter locates a suspected mine, the Mark V is launched and guided toward the unidentified object by sonar echoes corresponding to the object and the PAP transponder. The vehicle heading indication is displayed on the TV monitor, or on the display of the nearfield sonar.

The remotely-operated craft's speed is reduced when nearing the suspicious object, and a searchlight may be turned on to permit better identification by the TV camera. If the object turns out to be a ground mine, an explosive charge is dropped within two meters of the mine. The submersible is piloted back to the minehunting vessel. Once back on board, the 100-kg charge is detonated by the shock wave of a grenade thrown over the side of the mother ship.

If the object turns out to be a moored mine, the Mark V cutters are fastened to the mine cable. A small explosive charge ensures the line is severed. Thereafter, the procedure for disposing of the mine remains the same as with a ground mine.

Modern mine warfare is a battle of wits between the mine designer and the minehunter, with technology stealing the initiative. While NATO's European navies have made progress in modernizing their MCM force in recent years, major deficiencies still exist, observe various naval experts. They point out, for example, the construction of new mine countermeasures vessels has emphasized minehunters at the expense of minesweepers -- a policy that could have serious consequences. In a NATO-Warsaw Pact war, they reason, there would be many situations in which sweeping, not hunting, would be more effective in countering Soviet mines.

Added to this is the fact that newer Soviet technology has extended the mine threat to deeper waters, forcing NATO to develop the ability to sweep in these areas. Some naval analysts also perceive a technology gap in NATO's ability to counter the Soviets' advanced influence mines.

Then there is the matter of sheer numbers. "Our total MCM resources are simply inadequate when compared with the potential threat posed against us, not to mention the size and critical nature of our task," says Admiral Staveley.

Competing priorities for the protection of Western Europe will be a perennial problem within NATO, with resources spread thinly over everything from forward air defense and antitank warfare, to maintaining minimum levels of go-to-war stockpiles. "What's essential," says Admiral Staveley, "is that mine countermeasures continues to receive the high-level attention it deserves." IDI

"GREYHOUNDS OF THE SEAS"

AS FAST AS EVER, WITH A LOT MORE BITE

by Kirby J. Harrison

In the early days of World War I, the German U-boat menace threatened to choke the fragile lifeline between the U.S. and the Allies in Europe. From that threat was born a new kind of warship -- quick, agile, and capable of dealing with the submarine threat.

To the men who sailed in them and to those in the convoys they protected, they were beautiful. Sleek and fast, the destroyers and destroyer escorts were "The Greyhounds of the Seas."

Their progeny are alive and well in today's Navy. Still sleek and fast, they are more able than ever to defend themselves and the vessels in their charge.

The Navy has 219 ships whose ancestry is traced to those first destroyers and destroyer escorts. Now, as then, they are lighter ships designed to act as a defensive screen for carrier battle and surface action groups, amphibious assault actions, and merchant marine convoys.

The destroyerman of two previous world wars would still recognize the rakish cut of the bow and low silhouette, but he would hardly believe the size and firepower in this new breed.

Admiral Arleigh E. Burke is a destroyerman whose dashing exploits in World War II earned him the nickname "31-Knot Burke." In July 1986, 84-year-old Burke presided over the keel laying of a new class of destroyer that will bear his name. Still keen of eye and mind, he advised the men who will sail in those ships, "This ship is built to fight. You'd better know how."

The ships may be relatively small surface combatants. In battle, perhaps, they would be rated as underdogs. But Americans have always championed the underdog and are fond of pointing out, "It isn't the size of the dog in the fight, but the size of the fight in the dog."

There is plenty of fight in the Navy's "Greyhounds."

The largest of these ships are the cruisers. Little more than 550 feet long and averaging about 9,500 tons, they are just slightly smaller than the light cruisers of World War II. But they are still lightweights when compared to the supercarriers three football fields long, or to the 58,000-ton battleships IOWA, NEW JERSEY and MISSOURI. And it is interesting to note that until mid-1975, the present cruisers had been classified as destroyer leaders. Like the smaller destroyers (DDs and DLGs) and frigates (FFs and FFGs), the cruisers are armed to defend against air, surface and sub-surface attack. They are, however, considered by the Navy to be capable of independent surface action and have a primary role in antiaircraft defense.

In the multiple-threat world of naval warfare, versatility is a virtue. The new Ticonderoga class guided missile cruisers fairly bristle with versatility, with everything from standoff, rocket-launched homing torpedoes to surface-to-air missiles. Best of all, she and her sister ships have Aegis, a combat weapons system described without apology as, "...star wars at sea."

The key to the system is the AN/SPY-1 multi-function phased array radar, capable of simultaneous search, track and missile guidance functions, with a tracking capacity of well over 100 targets.

Unlike conventional radiating antennae that rotate through 360 degrees with a 12 to 24-second lapse, Aegis searches continuously through the hemisphere with hundreds of pencil-like beams under control of a digital computer. It is fast, accurate, and allows for multiple launch against multiple targets.

Perhaps few ships have been so severely criticized as the TICONDEROGA in her first year with the fleet. Critics wondered if the sailors manning her would be capable of operating and maintaining the high technology that is a critical part of the sophisticated weapons system. Detractors claimed she would be unable to cope with "stream raids" of missiles aimed at her. Some even alleged that she was so top-heavy she would capsize in extremely heavy weather.

That was five years ago. Since then, the TICONDEROGA and subsequent ships of the class have weathered rough seas and the critics' allegations quite handily.

On the TICONDEROGA's first patrol off Lebanon in 1984, her presence had such an impact, because of Aegis' successful detection, identification and tracking of aircraft, that air patrols were reduced. It was the YORKTOWN that provided the air

Scenes from "Tico" class cruisers (Clockwise from below) USS TICONDEROGA in the Mediterranean: HS-7 helicopter takes off from the TICONDEROGA, off the coast of Beirut: "AN/SPY-1" multi-function phased array radar: Quartermaster on the bridge: Combat Information Center on the USS VINCENNES.

intercept support for fighters to find the Egyptian airliner carrying the hijackers of the cruise ship ACHILLE LAURO. And both the YORKTOWN and VINCENNES were focal points of successful operations in the Gulf of Sidra which led to the sinking of at least two Libyan patrol boats, and to the strike against Libyan missile sites and other targets.

Congress was impressed enough to reverse its usual posture and actually add a third Aegis cruiser to President Reagan's request for two such ships in the fiscal year 1987 budget.

In addition to the Aegis-controlled STANDARD surface-to-air missile, the Ticonderoga class also carries the highly regarded Phalanx "Gatling" gun as a defense against rapidly closing enemy aircraft and antiship missiles.

With its own fire control radar, the six-barreled gun can track the target and fire 3,000 rounds a minute of 20mm/76 caliber, depleted uranium projectiles, two and one-half times heavier than steel.

The "Tico" class is also armed with the 5-inch/54 caliber gun. This semi-automatic antiaircraft weapon is extremely accurate against fast, maneuverable surface vessels and against shore targets, firing 16 to 20 rounds per minute. In addition to the Navy's new high fragmentation projectile, the 5-inch/54 will also fire the "smart" projectile expected to become operational in 1989. With laser guidance control and a rocket motor, the semi-active "smart" projectile can be guided to the target from the ship, from a shore installation or from an aircraft.

Also in the Ticonderoga arsenal is the reliable HARPOON surface-to-surface missile and rocket-launched homing torpedo (ASROC).

The newer ships of the Ticonderoga class are even faster on the draw. They carry the recently developed vertical launch system (VLS). And, in addition to being HARPOON capable, they also have the more powerful and longer range TOMAHAWK surface-to-surface missile.

Vertical launch has taken the "Greyhound" Navy into a new era in naval warfare. With VLS, there are no blind, non-firing zones. No time is wasted moving missiles to the launcher rail or training the launcher, and the ship does not need to be maneuvered to present the weapons battery to the target.

Aegis ships with VLS will carry launch modules forward and aft, with a possible mix of HARPOON, TOMAHAWK, and STANDARD weapons, totaling 122 rounds.

There are 26 other cruisers (CGNs and CGs), in addition to the Aegis class CGs. Perhaps the best known of these is the older BAINBRIDGE, the only ship in her class and the first of the nuclear-powered cruisers.

A notable advantage of the nuclear-powered cruisers is their ability to operate for extended periods without need of refueling. This was graphically demonstrated in 1964 when the BAINBRIDGE and LONG BEACH made an around-the-world cruise, escorting the nuclear-powered carrier ENTERPRISE.

The newest of the nuclear-powered cruisers are the six ships of the Virginia and California classes. Their armament is similar to that of the Kidd class.

The destroyer classes (DDs and DLGs) bear the most obvious resemblance to the old destroyers of World Wars I and II, though the 563-foot long Spruance class destroyers and Kidd class guided missile destroyers are almost twice the size of the old oil-burning escorts.

Both the Spruance and Kidd ships are highly automated, from the computerized gas turbine engine plants to the bridge. This automation has the added benefit of a 20 percent reduction in personnel over a similar ship with conventional systems.

Sailors on the Kidd somewhat tongue-in-cheek refer to their ship as the Ayatollah class. All four vessels of the Kidd class had been scheduled for delivery to Iran prior to the rise to power of the ruling Ayatollah Khomeni. When the order was canceled in 1979, a supplemental budget request resulted in the U.S. Navy's acquisition of what are de-

scribed as the most powerful destroyers in the fleet.

The primary role of the destroyer classes is that of antisubmarine warfare, and they are well fitted for the job. In addition to the latest bow-mounted sonar systems, some of the Spruance and Kidd ships are equipped with the newly developed long range detection tactical towed array sonar (TACTAS). This gives them an effective counter to increases in the range of weapons carried by Soviet submarines. Scheduled for installation aboard Spruance and

Kidd ships, as well as the Ticonderoga cruisers, Perry class guided missile frigates, and under-construction Burke guided missile destroyers, is the highly advanced SQQ-89 antisubmarine warfare system.

Plans also call for deployment of the new SH-60B Seahawk LAMPS Mk III on 100 surface vessels. They are already aboard the Kidd and Ticonderoga ships.

This additional antisubmarine warfare element greatly extends the defense umbrella of the battle group.

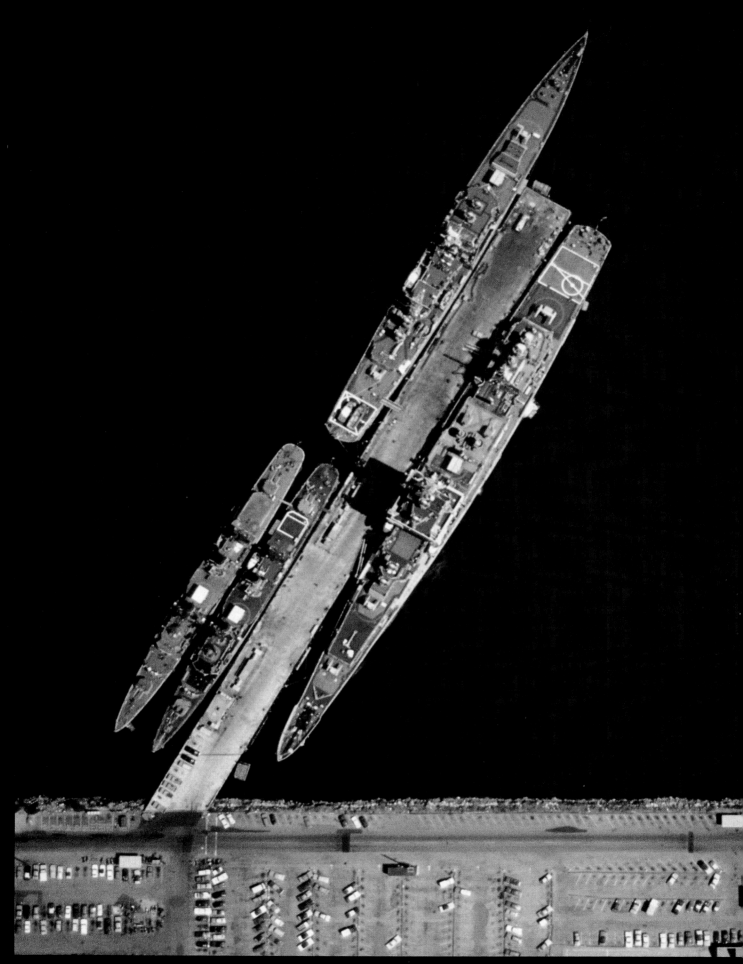

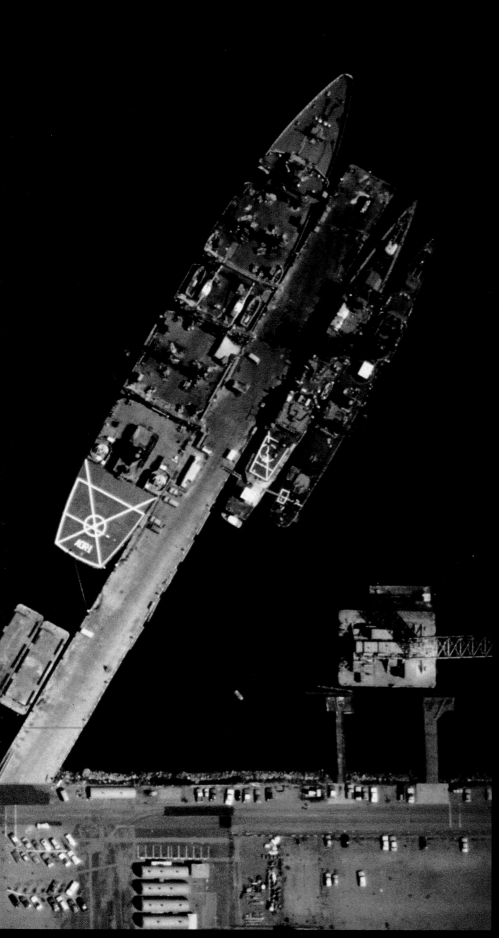

The most impressive new member of the destroyer classes is the Arleigh E. Burke, scheduled for delivery in 1990. Designed to replace the aging Adams and Farragut guided missile destroyer classes, the 466-foot long guided missile destroyers will feature Aegis, TOMAHAWK and VLS.

From the keel up, the Burke ships have been designed to incorporate the latest technology. The new hull form is designed to reduce vertical motion and allow higher speeds in heavier sea states. The Burke will have a "steel-space-steel" plating to protect vital spaces, and the ships will be all-steel construction. The VLS built into the ships will be compatible with all weapons upgrades anticipated throughout the construction period.

And to avoid the cost over-runs that commonly accompany annual capability upgrades, the Burke class will be built in "flights," permitting introduction of state-of-the-art technology at pre-planned points in the building program.

Vice Admiral Robert L. Walters, former Deputy Chief of Naval Operations for Surface Warfare, described the Burke class as the "classic destroyer."

The propulsion plant on the Burke class will be similar to the gas turbines of the Ticonderoga class. This low-maintenance engineering plant can take the ship from "cold iron" to full speed in approximately 12 minutes. It may not sound terribly fast to a drag-strip fan, but first time riders of ships with this 80,000-horsepower plant are quick to grasp the significance of the "subway" straps that hang from the overhead of the bridge.

Where the battle group goes, the submarines are sure to follow. And there you will also find the frigates, dashing about like angry wasps, sonar searching and ready to drop a rude message on any underwater intruder.

The backbone of the frigate classes (FFs and FFGs) is the newer Oliver Hazard Perry ships. Though nine ships short of the 60 requested, the Navy is nonetheless delighted with the program. Every one of the 41 ships delivered to date has come in on schedule and below cost.

"It is one of the best-managed shipbuilding programs in the Navy's history," says a spokesman at the Navy Office of Information.

Sixteen of these escorts are on duty with the Naval Reserve, lending impetus to the "One Navy" concept.

The Perry ships are armed with two sets of triple-tube launchers for the Mk 46 torpedo; surface-to-air STANDARD missiles; HARPOON (from the same launcher as STANDARD); a single, 80-round per minute, 76mm gun; and one 20mm Phalanx gun.

The successful EXOCET missile attack on the Perry class frigate USS STARK received much publicity. According to Navy sources, suggestions that the STARK and other U.S. warships are defenseless targets against this very accurate surface-skimming antiship missile are patently unfair and incorrect. Navy spokesman Lt. Ken Ross explains that, "since the missiles were not engaged (by the STARK's defenses), it is not appropriate to state that the missiles penetrated the ship's defenses.

"Technical assessment of the FFG-7 class combat systems state that the threat posed to STARK could, with high probability, be engaged and defeated."

Like the Spruance ships, the role of the Perry class in antisubmarine warfare is enhanced by the fact that nearly half these vessels already carry the SH-60B LAMPS Mk III helicopter. The others are fitted for the refurbished SH-2F Seasprite LAMPS Mk I helicopter. The original single hangar has been modified to two adjacent hangars to house two antisubmarine helicopters.

The Knox ships were originally classified as ocean escorts (DEs). The Knox class has an eight-cell launcher capable of firing ASROC and HARPOON, and will carry four TOMAHAWK surface-to-surface missiles.

Still looking towards a 600-ship Navy with 15 battle groups as a minimum level, the Navy is looking forward to newer and more capable additions to the "Greyhound" fleet.

The Arleigh E. Burke will nicely compliment the antiaircraft capabilities of the Ticonderoga cruisers and the antisubmarine effectiveness of the Spruance destroyers.

The growing inventory of TOMAHAWK missiles, with a nuclear warhead option, will give the escort vessels of the battle group a potent offensive punch. Former Chief of Naval Operations, Admiral Thomas B. Hayward, just before his retirement, emphasized the importance of continued development of standoff weapons like the TOMAHAWK.

"We have reached the point where there is more leverage in improving the weapon -- making it smarter, longer legged and more capable of self-direction -- than in trying to achieve equivalent results through improvement of the launch platform (ship), " said Hayward.

The Navy sees a bright future with the Aegis-equipped Ticonderoga class. Ten of the Aegis cruisers are already operational and another two will be delivered this year. The minimum force objective is 27 ships of this class, of which 22 will have VLS.

The "Greyhound" Navy will play an increasingly important role in antisubmarine warfare in the coming years as part of a "layered strategy" for countering the Soviet submarine threat.

Using this strategy, the cruisers, destroyers and frigates would, as in past conflicts, form the main line of defense in protecting the battle group.

Soviet doctrine, according to U.S. Navy strategists, gives high priority to locating and destroying western sea-based nuclear assets, especially the carriers, ballistic missile submarines and TOMAHAWK-equipped ships.

U.S. Navy strategy, they add, consists of "...forcing the Soviet Union to face a most unpalatable and deterring prospect; that any conventional war they initiate with the west could be protracted, global and fought by a unified alliance in places and ways not necessarily of their choosing."

The success of that strategy is dependent on flexibility and mobility -- critical to effective screening forces.

In 1778, when the U.S. Navy was being born, a young captain anxiously sought a vessel to take against the enemy. His preference in ships was brief and to the point: "I do not wish to be associated with any ship that is not fast," said John Paul Jones, "for I intend to go in harm's way."

He, like "31-Knot Burke," would have been delighted with today's "Greyhound" Navy -- built fast to go in harm's way. IDI

UNITED STATES COAST GUARD

FIGHTING THE DRUG WARS

by Keith Jacobs

95304

High technology is now supplementing the long years of human experience gained by the U.S. Coast Guard (USCG) in "fighting the drug wars" and illegal immigration into the U.S.

The "drug war" has changed a lot in the last decade. In the mid-1970s, it was primarily American citizens with U.S.-registered yachts doing most of the importing of marijuana from Jamaica and Mexico into the United States. Today, it's foreign nationals, most often from the country of greatest export -- Colombia, with 75 percent of the world's cocaine -- with stolen yachts, "motherships" (trawlers, small merchant ships and large fishing craft), and often with stolen aircraft and a whole range of new smuggling methods and organizations.

Anyone who knows "street value" cocaine and marijuana knows it only takes a small investment to create millions of dollars of profit for those involved in the illegal trafficking. Estimates of cocaine available for export to the U.S. in 1986 was 306-307 tons, while marijuana totalled upwards of 9,000 tons. Mexico is now emerging as the primary source of marijuana being smuggled into the U.S., while a growing number of "motherships" are increasingly being used to haul large tonnages to at-sea off-loading sites allowing smaller craft (sailing and small boats) to make the final trip into U.S. harbors and hidden coastal enclaves. Such large shipments often originate off the northern Colombian coast (Guajira Peninsula) and may not unload until they have reached the coast of Massachusetts or, if loaded on Colombia's West Coast, will transit along the Pacific Coast as far north as the states of Oregon and Washington.

To fight the drug wars and handle other Coast Guard responsibilities (boating

HU-25A GUARDIAN

safety, environmental responses, ice and marine navigation, marine licensing, law enforcement) under the Department of Transportation (DOT), Congress is budgeting $2.74 billion in Fiscal Year 1988, in support of the 38,500-plus personnel now manning the ships, aircraft, and shore stations of the agency. The ships of the Coast Guard can be considered the 12th largest "navy" in the world. The aviation component makes it the 7th largest "air force" in the world! USCG ships and boats total over 240. Coast Guard Aviation manages some 225-plus aircraft and helicopters. As the Coast

Guard's overall war against drugs escalates, so does the cost -- from $226 million in 1981 to $445 million for 1986.

COORDINATED ZONE STRATEGY

The Coast Guard has organized what it calls the "Coordinated Zone Strategy" to defeat illegal drug smuggling. USCG handles Exclusive Economic Zone (EEZ) areas, out to 200 nautical miles (nm), while U.S. Customs handles overland interdiction. Customs coordinates the overall interdiction mission from Washington, DC.

Each smuggling route is divided into three distinct zones:
 Departure Zone -- an area adjacent to foreign shores.
Transit Zone -- enroute areas, including Caribbean "choke points" for USCG interdiction efforts.
Arrival Zone -- coastal areas adjacent to U.S. soil and where final smuggling and/or transshipment efforts take place.
 To implement the USCG strategy, several major programs and organizations have been established.

Coast Guard Law Enforcement Detachments (LEDETS) are deployed onboard U.S. Navy ships for purposes of boarding seized and suspected vessels on the high seas. Detachments are now located in San Diego, San Francisco, and Miami.

A USCG squadron of three 146-ton Sea Bird class surface effect ships (WSWS), are stationed at Key West, Florida, for high-speed (30 knots-plus) interdiction missions.

A major USCG cutter has been stationed off the Yucatan Peninsula to aid the location and monitoring of vessels out of Mexico.

A U.S. Navy squadron of six hydrofoil fast attack craft (PHM) stationed at Key West now carry LEDETS onboard.

Through NNBIS, Department of Defense (DoD) assets are used to supplement Coast Guard resources for maritime and airborne surveillance. Coverage extends from the Panama Canal to Maine, Alaska, and westward to Hawaii.

An Intelligence Coordination Center (ICC) in Washington, DC and regional ICCs, plus analysis offices in San Francisco and New York, handle inter-agency intelligence information (supplementing NNBIS locations).

A new Command Center (with C3I capabilities) is being built in Miami to handle Gulf and Caribbean areas.

In ships and personal hardware, impressive gains are being made with regard to using high-technology equipment to take the advantage away from drug smugglers. These include:

-- providing copilots of HU-25 Falcon surveillance aircraft with Aerojet General Electro Systems Divison "Aireye" multisensor systems. This combines side looking airborne radar (SLAR) with an Active Gated Television (AGTV) low light television system for adverse weather and a laser illuminator for night vision, plus a KS-87B optical camera system.

-- four new Fast Coastal Interceptors (FCIs), a 43-foot high-speed, light craft designed after ocean-racing boats. These new "43-series" craft will give seaborne Coast Guard personnel the ability to run down suspected craft, often a difficult task with existing harbor craft and larger ocean-going cutters.

-- modernizing larger 378-foot WMECs which already carry a HH-3F or HH-52A heavy helicopter. These will be fitted with RGM-84 HARPOON antiship missiles. Further orders for "Famous/Bear" class 270-foot medium endurance cutters (four more due in 1988/89); and, buying a total of 37

Island class 110-foot harbor cutter and patrol craft, which have a five-day offshore patrol capability. Four are already assigned at Miami, five at Roosevelt Roads, Puerto Rico, and numerous others are individually assigned throughout the U.S. to replace older, and slower, 82-foot Cape class craft.

AVIATION IMPROVEMENTS

In related Coast Guard Aviation developments, high-tech is replacing the old "Coasty" watching the seas with binoculars from an aircraft observation bubble.

On order are 96 Aerospatiale HH-65 Dolphin short-range helos, with about 50 already delivered. Minimum equipment fitted to the HH-65s exceeds anything previously packaged into one helicopter of this size. Cruise speed is 130 knots, with normal radius of 150 nm for up to three hours endurance. The shrouded tail rotor makes the Dolphin easily recognizable, along with the turbine whine of its Avco Lycoming LTS101-75B-2 turboshaft engines. Onboard avionics include Collins Avionics Group and Rockwell International equipment. Top speed is 165 knots. Copilots are getting the Litton night-vision goggles.

By the summer of 1988, all air stations with HH-52 Sea Guards will have HH-65 replacements. The French Aerospatiale-designed helo is being built in Grand Prairie, Texas.

As part of a recently announced cooperative effort between the office of the Deputy Assistant Secretary of Defense for Drug Policy Enforcement and the DoD Task Force on Drug Enforcement, the USCG has obtained 12 Sikorsky UH-60A BlackHawk helicopters and two Grumman E-2C Hawkeyes.

Older Hercules C-130s are being replaced by 16 new Lockheed HC-130H Hercules turboprop aircraft. The HC-130Hs can exceed 2,600 nm or an endurance up to 14 hours, becoming the long-range workhorses of the USCG. The "Aireye" system is being installed in these new aircraft. This system was designed to help the Coast Guard carry out law enforcement and SAR missions in a more effective manner, basing it on Aerojet General's Airborne Ocean Surveillance Syetems (AOSS).

Two Grumman E-2C Hawkeye airborne early-warning aircraft (AWACS) have been added. The $25 million aircraft entered service in February 1987. They are operated by a new Coast Guard unit out of Norfolk Naval Air Station, Virginia, covering the Caribbean at

altitudes of nearly 20,000 feet. Emphasis remains on coverage of the Windward Passage and other Caribbean "choke points" on the drug route north.

Once airborne detections are made, a faster HU-25 is sent out from its "alert" status under E-2C control. The intercept is coordinated by the E-2C, often at night. If the intercepted aircraft flies without lights, it is difficult to intercept and keep in contact. With the aid of the E-2C's radars, even evasive maneuvers can be tracked, allowing an intercepting Falcon to be directed to the intruder. With the aid of Litton night-vision goggles, the Falcon's copilot can track the unidentified aircraft and force it to land. Customs handles apprehension after the intercept.

True "air intercept" radars have been added to some HU-25 Falcons. Eight HU-25As will receive airborne search and track radars modified from those carried on the U.S. Air Force F-16. These radars provide outstanding airborne coordination and tracking capabilities.

CATCHING THEM'S GETTING HARDER

After 1982, a year in which record drug intercepts were made by various law enforcement agencies, there was a large drop in marijuana seizures, partly due to drug dealers changing tactics. Hidden compartments in yachts and other vessels became more prevalent, and greater use of Caribbean eastern passes was made by larger vessels. Because of hidden compartments, the Coast Guard and others are forced to spend more time searching stopped vessels.

In 1984, increased resources became available to aid the war on drugs: SES craft and "Aerostat" tethered balloons, plus increased U.S. Navy cooperation and the establishment of 13 Organized Crime Drug Enforcement Task Forces (OCDETF). Arrests climbed.

The impact of NNBIS and establishment of the Intelligence Coordination Center (ICC) in past years began to be recognized, as the largest number of cases and vessels were seized in 1984-85. Operations and intelligence efforts were increasingly being focused further away from U.S. shores by 1985, resulting in greatly expanded intelligence gathering -- including information implicating senior Panamanian and Nicaraguan officials' involvement in drug smuggling operations. Smugglers even tried to use a tug and barge towing method to bring in large quantities on a single trip; discovery quickly ended such brash efforts!

Seizures were so low in 1985 that some felt organized drug supply groups were attempting a "wait and see" attitude -- maybe combined with poor crop results

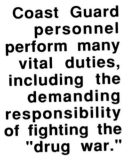

Coast Guard personnel perform many vital duties, including the demanding responsibility of fighting the "drug war."

for the year -- hoping the rise in drug enforcement would taper off. It didn't.

It also may have been related to switching to cocaine, as the rising star of drug smugglers. Quantities of cocaine seized increased nearly 60 percent -- exceeding 10,000 lbs. Increased marijuana crop destruction by Colombian police and other military forces began to reduce marijuana exports out of that country, while increased sources of the drug were beginning to flood out of Mexico.

Great quantities of marijuana were also being grown in northern California, Oregon, and elsewhere in the Northwest, easing reliance on overseas imports. Maritime marijuana smuggling has declined from overseas sources during 1987.

Last year, Customs took over direction of The Interdiction Committee (TIC) in Washington. The Coast Guard, however, remains the lead agency for maritime enforcement. The cycle of operations in an effectively coordinated law enforcement operation involves first detection of an airborne or maritime smuggler. This may

be by the USCG's new E-2Cs, by DoD or Federal Aviation Administration (FAA) ground-based radars, or the new Aerostats employed by Customs. The Joint C3 Center then aids in classifying the intruder as a likely smuggler or not, and begins the intercept portion of the coordinated effort. This might entail dispatch of high-speed HU-25A Falcon jets, or diversion of other aircraft or helicopter(s) into an area where the intruder might be observed and monitored. Once stopped, the vessel or aircraft can then be boarded and inspected.

The final apprehension has not always been easily accomplished. It was common for drug-smuggling aircraft to drop their loads at sea, in the swamps of the Southeast, or in other isolated areas in order to land clean after being successfully intercepted. Helicopters of the HH-52 type were unable to race along with the smugglers' aircraft, which range in size from Beechcraft and Pipers to such large aircraft as DC-3 and DC-4/-6 types. Enter the jet Falcons and this changed the nature of the

game. The Falcon can chase even the best of them!

Better coordination and navigational aids make it possible to get a fix on dumping operations by the drug-carrying aircraft, so these marijuana loads can be picked up by law enforcement personnel long after the dumping. Those dumps can now be seen during the act by the copilot using Litton night-vision goggles, and picked up at sea by U.S. Navy vessels with LEDETS or diving teams onboard. The new Aireye system will provide a video record for criminal prosecution of aircraft and ship operators engaged in dumping operations. As the saying goes, "Once you hook-em, you got to still bring-em in!"

As with faster jets, the new Fast Interceptor Craft (FIC), a 43-foot "cigarette" boat design, provides the speed with which to catch many of the marine violators, who have also adopted similar high-speed small craft designs for coastal operations. The seven-ton craft are built by Tempest Marine, North Miami Beach, Florida.

The first four craft, reported to cost $330,000 for the order, are powered by two Caterpillar 3208-TA diesels developing 375 brake horsepower (bhp). Twin shafts offer fine maneuverability at low speed. As BMC Richard Gregory (USCG) stated, "While I can't give you the top speed, I will say it does better than 50 knots. These are the fastest standard boats in the Coast Guard."

The first "43 Class" boat arrived at Base Miami in April 1987; another is stationed at Fort Lauderdale, Florida. Station Islamorada is slated to get one also. Crewmembers for the FCIs were handpicked for their familiarity with the area and maritime law enforcement backgrounds.

It should be evident the Coast Guard is entering a whole new era of high-technology law enforcement. The Coast Guard has the professionals; now it's getting the equipment to expand the war on drug smuggling. With Congressional budgetary support, innovative ideas such as the Vice-President's NNBIS staff and regional centers program, inter-agency cooperation, and Navy assists on drug intercepts have resulted in seizure of 72 vessels. This has netted 1.5 million pounds of marijuana and 1,000 pounds of cocaine -- (plus 428 arrests).

These and other efforts will make the cost of doing business too high for drug dealers, and the "good guys" may once more gain the upper hand in the "drug wars." IDI

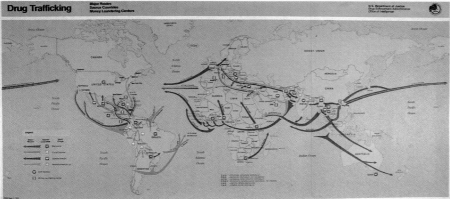

HH-65A DOLPHIN

OMNI-DIRECTIONAL
AIR DATA SYSTEM (OADS)

STARFLEX ROTOR HEAD
HINGELESS-LIGHTWEIGHT

GRAPHITE/EPOXY
COMPOSITE ROTOR BLADES

RESCUE HOIST
WITH OPERATOR
STAND-UP CAPABILITY

CLEAR CABIN SPACE
FOR MISSION VERSATILITY
CABIN VOLUME - 236 CU. FT.

EXCELLENT CREW
VISIBILITY FOR SEARCH
AND RESCUE OPERATIONS

20g CRASH PROTECTION
FOR CREW AND PASSENGERS

PLANNAR ARRAY WEATHER
AND SEARCH RADAR

EMERGENCY FLOTATION BAGS
FOR STABLE SEA STATE 5 FLOTATION

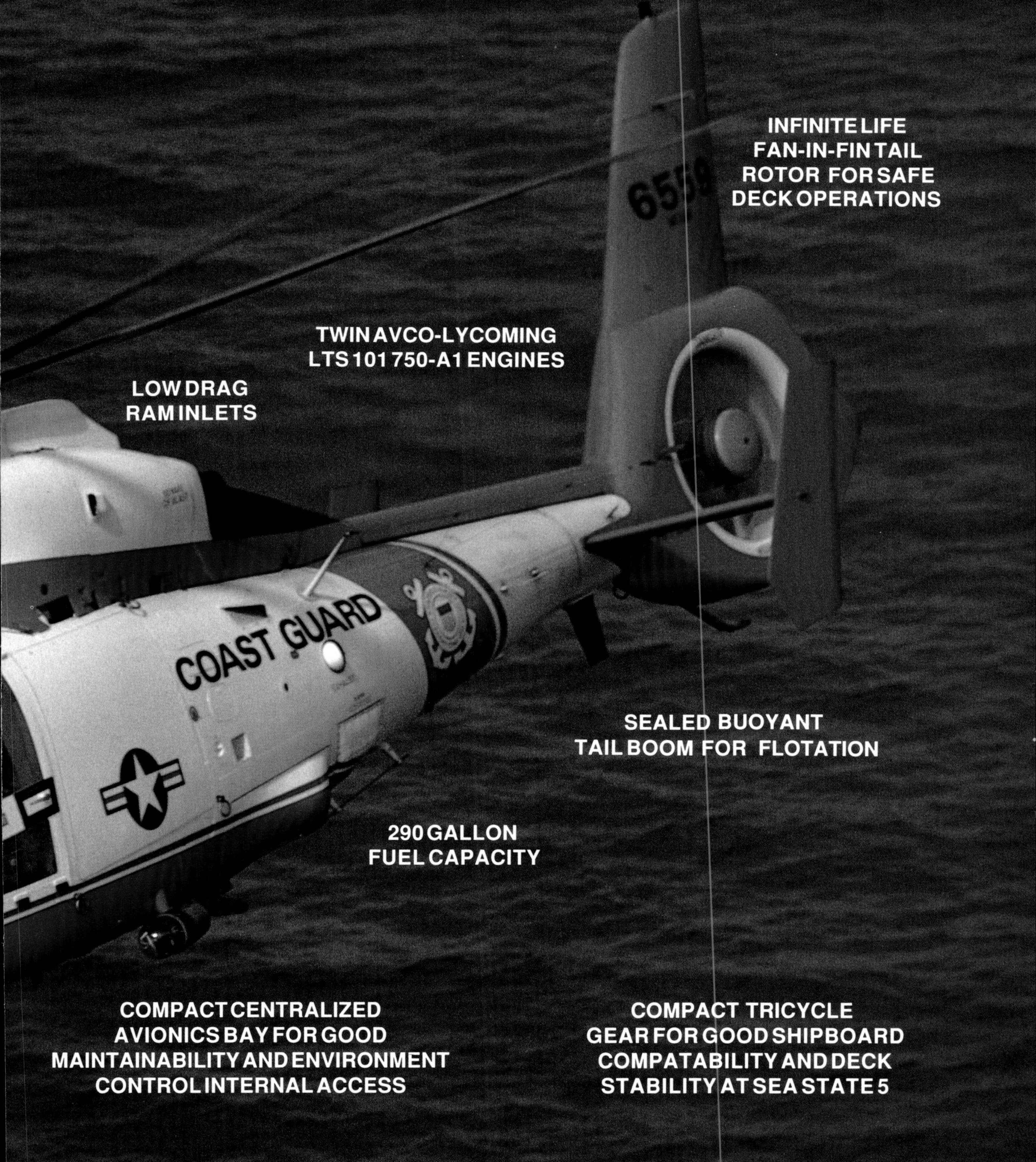

INFINITE LIFE
FAN-IN-FIN TAIL
ROTOR FOR SAFE
DECK OPERATIONS

TWIN AVCO-LYCOMING
LTS 101 750-A1 ENGINES

LOW DRAG
RAM INLETS

6559

COAST GUARD

SEALED BUOYANT
TAIL BOOM FOR FLOTATION

290 GALLON
FUEL CAPACITY

COMPACT CENTRALIZED
AVIONICS BAY FOR GOOD
MAINTAINABILITY AND ENVIRONMENT
CONTROL INTERNAL ACCESS

COMPACT TRICYCLE
GEAR FOR GOOD SHIPBOARD
COMPATABILITY AND DECK
STABILITY AT SEA STATE 5

© HANK CARUSO 1988   US COAST GUARD HH-65 DOLPHIN

54

SILENT STALKERS

By Damian Housman

The world of the submarine is quiet and deadly. There can be no doubt that the next war may be decided by how well our submarine designers and crews do their job. If they have done it well enough, there may not be a next war, at least not between the Soviet Union and the United States.

More than 70 percent of the world is covered by water, which gives navies a vast expanse in which to work. Some naval forces perform a vital peacetime function through their visibility. The presence of a carrier battle group in the area gives a feeling of comfort to friends and allies. At the same time, potential enemies must continue to ponder the possible results of hostile action. That is one way surface ships deter war.

The submarine deters in quite another way. Whether it is an attack submarine or a ballistic missile submarine, its job is to remain hidden. Virtually silent and invisible, submarines deter because the potential aggressor knows what damage they can inflict, and knows how unlikely it is that they can be located and destroyed before launching at least some of their devastating weapons.

The World War II allies were extremely fortunate that Germany recognized too late the value of the submarine. With a relative handful of U-boats, the German Navy interdicted massive amounts of supplies destined for Britain and the Soviet Union. The British were on subsistence rations for the duration of the war, thanks to the success of these underwater wolf packs. The resupplying of Britain would have been immeasurably more difficult if the Germans had invested in more submarines, rather than in cruisers and battleships.

The Soviets have been excellent students of warfare, and they appreciate key elements of naval warfare such as the submarine. Their submarine fleet today approaches 400, including more than 300 attack subs. Of their attack force, which includes 35 classes of torpedo, cruise missile, and auxilliary subs, about half are nuclear powered -- with the percentage on the increase. Their ballistic missile submarine force (SSBN), which numbers some 61 boats, carries a total of 916 nuclear armed missiles, according to the Pentagon's **Soviet Military Power 1987**. This does not include several older Golf II, Golf III, and Hotel III SSBNs, which carry weapons unsuitable for the strategic mission, but are lethally effective for theater or tactical missions.

The past 10 years have seen a revolution in Soviet ballistic missile submarine construction. During that time, 21 SSBNs have been built, carrying a total of 352 multiple warhead missiles. Before their appearance, Soviet subs carried only single warhead missiles. Today, more than 3,000 reentry vehicles (RVs) have been deployed aboard Soviet submarines, more than triple the total of 10 years ago. The missiles which carry

these RVs are larger, more accurate, and have far greater range than their predecessors.

The Soviets have launched four new Delta IV class subs, with two more believed to be under construction. Each carries 16 of the brand new SS-N-23 ballistic missiles, which can launch 10 warheads to a range of 8,300 kilometers (km). The slightly shorter Delta III carried the same number of SS-N-18s, which had fewer warheads and a shorter range.

The SSBN that has generated the most comment over the last few years is the Typhoon class. Six of these monsters have already been launched, with two or three more believed to be under construction. The world's largest submarine at 25,000 metric tons displacement, each Typhoon carries 20 SS-N-20 ballistic missiles, which have six to nine warheads and a range equal to that of the SS-N-23.

Soviet modernization efforts have changed the strategic equation. With missiles of longer range, their SSBNs no longer need to patrol so far from home. Some can retain their ability to target the continental U.S. while in their home ports. This greatly complicates the job of our attack submarines, which now have to search a greater area of ocean to find Soviet SSBNs, and must venture ever closer to Soviet waters. Killing Soviet SSBNs is a mission, therefore, with a great deal of risk.

Soviet SSBNs are expected to deploy to "bastions," areas near the Soviet land mass. Concentrating them in these areas may seem like it invites their destruction by U.S. attack subs, but it also allows concentration of Soviet forces to

protect them. Most Soviet surface ships have been designed principally for the ASW mission, and they will have a large role to play in keeping our attack subs away. So will Soviet attack subs, and land-based air. Getting through that gauntlet to reach the bastions, whether through the Greenland-Iceland-United Kingdom (GIUK) Gap, or under the Arctic icecap, will be extremely difficult.

No less impressive than the Soviet SSBN force is their emerging attack submarine capability. Currently producing nine different classes of attack subs, the Soviets are making rapid progress in propulsion, weapons and, most ominous of all, in quieting their boats to make detection far more difficult.

It is difficult to know precisely how the Soviets evolved from building "underwater noise machines" to building sophisticated, fast, powerful, and very quiet submarines. Many Western experts believe that espionage and "improper" technology transfer had a lot to do with it. Media accounts of the

Walker-Whitworth spy ring suggest the Soviets obtained war-winning information concerning U.S. ASW capabilities, including the frequencies our forces monitor which give away Soviet submarine positions. This has led to revised operating procedures on their part, as well as changes in submarine design.

The sale of large scale four and nine axis milling machines to the Soviets by Japan's Toshiba Corp., together with software for operating the machinery from Norway's Kongsberg Vaapenfabrikk, is suspected of providing the Soviets with the means of producing much quieter submarine propellers. To be sure, the last four classes of Soviet attack submarines have been far quieter than any of their predecessors.

On the other hand, the Soviets have developed several decades of operational experience with submarines, and are fully capable of technological improvements of their own. Their subs were already getting quieter, thanks to better sound insulation, better reactor and hull design, and anechoic coatings. It is likely that the Toshiba-Kongsberg transfer simply accelerated what was going to happen in any case some time in the near future. Nonetheless, some critics have taken to call the latest Soviet attack class sub, the Akula, by the name of the Toshiba-class.

With the advent of the nuclear submarine, the requirement for mass storage of diesel fuel permitted the elimination of the outer of the two hulls previously found on all submarines. The U.S. has used single (pressure) hulls on all its subs since. The Soviets, on the other hand, have retained the double hull configuration. There are trade-offs. There is a greater problem with corrosion in a double hull sub, greater weight for a given volume, and poor crew habitability.

On the other hand, double hulled subs are more survivable when damaged in battle, have greater reserve buoyancy, less drag, and can use the inner-hull standoff distance for additional equipment. The pressure hull also has better protection from the effects of colliding with surface or subsurface craft, or grounding. Considering the frequency with which Soviet subs have been colliding with other objects, that is not an insignificant benefit.

In keeping with their task of protecting the strategic missile sub force, most Soviet SSNs are equipped with torpedoes and antisubmarine missiles. Though it is believed that Soviet passive underwater sound detection capability still lags behind ours, it must be assumed that the Soviets have the equipment to do the job. Recent classes of Soviet SSNs have what appears to be a pod on the vertical tail fin, which may hold a towed array sensor together with its cable and associated gear. Towing an array places it away from the subs own noise sources, thus greatly increasing detection effectiveness.

While U.S. subs tend to be jacks-of-all-trades, Soviet subs are designed for very specific uses. Several classes, such as Charlie II and Oscar, have antiship missiles in addition to their torpedoes. These vessels are suitable for attacking surface ships, such as U.S. carrier battle groups. It is not expected that a Soviet sub alone would attack an American CVBG. It is far more likely to be a combined attack, utilizing land-based bombers, surface ships, and several submarines. The idea is to present the defending battle group with so many incoming missiles at one time that some will inevitably get through.

The SS-N-9 missiles of the Charlie II and the SS-N-19s of the Oscar, together with the SS-N-12s of the Echo II, are designed to fly fast and low to minimize reaction time.

Torpedo attacks can be expected as well, though one might think that getting that close to an American aircraft carrier is impossible... possibly not. The Soviets are building some extremely fast attack subs, including some with extraordinary depth capability. Their steel-hulled boats can already run well below our own subs, but the Soviets also have several titanium-hulled subs which can go much deeper. Some experts suggest a Soviet sub can hide deep in the ocean while awaiting its chance to strike, then run full speed at the target ship. True, a sub at high speed is easy to detect, but the speeds of some Soviet subs are such that they can be in firing position before our ASW forces can respond. And, a high strength titanium hull may survive a hit from a standard Mk 46 torpedo, even if the torpedo can catch the sub.

If all this demonstrates the serious-ness of the Soviet submarine threat, it should not be seen as a hopeless situa-tion. The U.S. still has some considerable advantages in the undersea war.

Our sea-based strategic deterrent force resides aboard our ballistic missile submarines. By mid-1987, the U.S. had 38 SSBNs of both the Poseidon and Tri-dent (Ohio class) type. Together, the Po-seidon types have 448 launchers for Po-seidon (C-3) and Trident I (C-4) missiles. The 10-warhead C-3 has a range of 4,000 km, while the eight-warhead C-4 has a range of 7,400 km. The Ohio class has 192 tubes for Trident I missiles, which next year will begin to be upgraded to the Lockheed Trident II (D-5) missile.

The Trident II missile will have a range about 50 percent greater than Trident I, carry 10-14 warheads with a yield as high as 600 kilotons, and will be the first sub-launched missiles large enough and accu-rate enough to knock out hard targets such as missile silos and command bunk-ers. Each Ohio class sub, built by Gener-al Dynamics Electric Boat Division, has 24 launch tubes, making the Trident the biggest, least vulnerable, deterent force we have.

Our 10 older Polaris subs have been retired or reconfigured to an attack or transport role. Twelve of the 31 Poseidon subs now carry Lockheed Trident I mis-siles. There are now eight Ohio class subs in service, with a total construction program of between 20 and 25 currently being called for.

Nearly 100 attack submarines are in the U.S. fleet, including boats of the Per-mit, Skate, Skipjack, Narwhal, Glenard P. Lipscomb, Ethan Allen (converted SSBN), and Los Angeles (SSN-688) classes. Of these, the most significant in terms of numbers and capability is the Los An-geles class, built by General Dynamics Electric Boat Division and Newport News Shipbuilding. With a top speed of more than 30 knots and a displacement of about 6,500 metric tons, the SSN-688s are nearly 10,000 tons smaller than the Soviet Oscars. Nonetheless, the SSN-688 is significantly quieter than its recent Soviet counterpart, and far stealthier than older Soviet boats.

The Los Angeles comes well armed. The Mk 48 heavy, wire-guided torpedo is thought by many to be the best in the world, with extremely long range and ex-cellent target finding abilities, even in an electronic countermeasures environment. Because of the impressive operational capabilities of some fast, deep diving So-viet attack boats (such as Alfa), the Mk 48 ADCAP program was begun to improve the torpedo still further. Another standoff

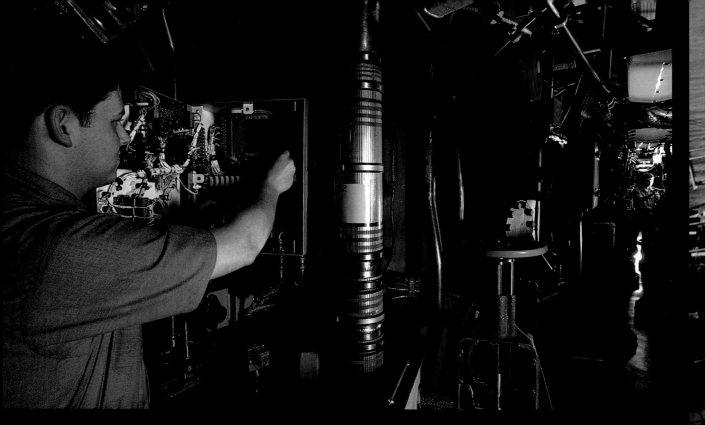

ASW weapon on board is the SUBROC ASW rocket.

For attacking surface ships, McDonnell Douglas' HARPOON is the standard weapon, with a range of 60 nautical miles (nm), and a combat-earned reputation for hitting with devastating effects. For much longer ranges, out to several hundred miles, the TOMAHAWK cruise missile is useful against both ships and and targets.

All submarines are space limited, and the addition of capabilities such as TOMAHAWK have stretched space aboard Los Angeles to the limit and beyond. There is only so much room for torpedoes and missiles, and only four torpedo tubes. Therefore, the Navy has begun to modify some of these submarines with 12 Vertical Launch System (VLS) tubes, mounted outside the pressure hull. They will carry TOMAHAWK missiles, and will have free space inside for more torpedoes and HARPOONS.

It is the problem of space limitation that is driving the U.S. Navy to design a new class of attack sub. There is no doubt that the Los Angeles is the finest ASW platform in the world today. However, sensor, computer fire control, data processing, and weaponry have reached their limit within the confines of the SSN-688 hull.

A new class of attack submarine, Sea Wolf, is on the way, incorporating far more advanced sensors than are possible inside the Los Angeles. In the meantime, the Navy intends to buy 27 SSN-688s with advanced capabilities. In addition to the VLS, the new subs will incorporate the IBM AN/BSY-2 combat system, which is too large to fit in the Los Angeles class. Another sensor improvement is the use of a passive wide aperture sonar array mounted on the side of the boat. The system will use fiber optics to link it with the fire control system. Overall, it will triple the combat effectiveness of Sea Wolf over the improved Los Angeles.

Other improvements will include eight torpedo tubes, each larger in size than the four on the SSN-688. In addition to Hughes Aircraft and Gould Inc. Mk 48 ADCAP torpedoes, it will use the new Boeing SEA LANCE long range standoff ASW weapon. Similar in concept to SUBROC, SEA LANCE uses a rocket to propel a Honeywell Mk 50 torpedo several miles through the air. It drops into the water and then acoustically searches for the enemy submarine.

Outnumbered by Soviet submarines more than three to one, our attack subs use superior tactics, geostrategic thinking, and technology to gain the combat edge. Even that would not be enough if it were not for the other resources our subs count on to locate and destroy the enemy. Satellites tell us of ship movements on the surface and in and out of ports. Fixed underwater sound systems, like SOSUS, detect subs at long range, and alert us to their presence.

Because of Soviet advances in acoustic countermeasures, other systems, like the T-AGOS passive sonar ships, augment SOSUS. Eventually, fiber optic-based systems will make evasion more difficult.

Land-based ASW patrol aircraft (P-3) are directed to a general location, and can quickly find and attack a submarine. In the case of a carrier battle group, a combination of towed sonar arrays, variable depth sonars, and active hull-mounted sonars are used by surface ships, while the CVBG also uses fixed-wing (S-3) and rotary aircraft to track, pinpoint, and attack approaching subs. Finally, there are the ships and submarines of our NATO allies, mostly conventionally powered, which relieve us to a great extent from using our own subs in several important areas.

Daily activities aboard the submarine USS CINCINNATI
(SSN 693), (clockwise from top left), sub commander peers
through the periscope; navigator plots the boat's course as another crewman scans the surface above; ship's officer
conducts emergency evacuation seminar; crewman relaxes
on his bunk alongside torpedo storage racks

The undersea war cannot be simplified, however, into a technology versus numbers equation. Both sides have technological advantages which they will exploit. There are also geographical considerations, such as natural chokepoints, and the Arctic icecap. Submarines hunting each other under the ice face a daunting game of hide and seek in which the stakes are high and the risks are huge. A quiet diesel sub can lurk amidst the ice, above the approaching SSN, to pounce unexpectedly. The fact that some Soviet SSBNs have been seen to punch through Arctic ice to provide a path for their ballistic missiles makes this an increasingly important aspect of submarine warfare.

The U.S. Navy must continue to improve its submarine and ASW capabilities. Failing to do so would place in jeopardy the credibility of our strategic deterrent, and our ability to transport our forces to Europe and Asia in case of war. The fact that we continue to maintain our lead under the seas is a clear message to the Soviets that we recognize the importance of submarine warfare, and have no intention of becoming second best. IDI

FRANCE'S CARRIER FORCE:
"NAVAL DISSUASION"

by Keith Jacobs

France has two conventional attack aircraft carriers in service and construction has begun on a new nuclear-powered attack carrier for the mid-1990s. Today, the two 32,000-ton Clemenceau class CVs -- flying Super Etendard IV attack aircraft and F-8E (FN) Crusader fighters -- form the backbone of what might be termed the naval portion of the nation's policy of "nuclear and conventional dissuasion."

In recent years, France has increased its associations with the North Atlantic Treaty Organization (NATO), though the nation continues to follow an independent course in regard to political and military policies. This often proves to the advantage of the United States and NATO nations, which have frequently been reluctant to conduct military operations against certain countries astride the shores of the Mediterranean, in the Middle East, and the Indian Ocean area.

During Lebanon's internal fighting in late1983, the French deployed the aircraft carrier FOCH to the Eastern Mediterranean as part of Operation Oliphant -- supporting the French contingent of United Nations (UN) peacekeeping forces in Lebanon. When French ground troops came under attack in early September, Super Etendard IV-Ps of squadron 16F began reconnaissance missions over Lebanon. On 22 September, a flight of four Super Etendard IVs -- supported by a flight of LTV F-8E (FN) Crusader fighters -- was launched against four Druze militia gun batteries that had been firing on Beirut city positions. The four artillery batteries attacked were located 12 miles (20 kilometers) east of Beirut. It was the first Aeronavale combat mission since the end of the Algerian War in the 1960s.

FRENCH DOCTRINE

In November 1959, then President Charles De Gaulle addressed the French Ecole Militaire, stating in part that the Republic "had as its raison d'etre...the defense of the nation's independence and integrity. It was necessary that the defense of France be French." He end-

ed the Algerian War and attempted to create a European political "third force" amid great controversy, with the latter to serve as the political basis of an independent French military force. His defense policies -- which included creation of a nuclear-armed force -- were designed to sustain French political initiatives.

The "doctrine of dissuasion" required deployment of enough nuclear weapons to inflict destruction equal to or greater than the stake which France might represent to an aggressor. "Dissuasion defense" was a "countervalue" strategy designed, not to inflict massive nuclear destruction on an aggressor, but to be the equivalent of tearing his arm off! France could not afford massive nuclear forces, but the creation of a limited nuclear force provided a sanctuary from direct nuclear attack -- its only threat being from the Soviet Union. It also allowed De Gaulle to rebuild French military forces from a largely civil guard and counter-insurgency force to one designed along modern lines and intended to operate largely on the European continent.

French dissuasion policies are based on three levels of force: strategic nuclear; tactical nuclear; and conventional forces. As former Minister Charles Hernu noted, the country's strategic nuclear force was designed "to dissuade all significant aggression against France and its vital interests." Tactical nuclear forces are intended to bridge the gap between strategic forces (IRBM, SLBM, and Mirage IV-A bombers, and conventional forces).

The French Navy's component of tactical nuclear forces is based on the two Clemenceau class carriers. French Air Force tactical nuclear-strike aircraft are based in northeast France and are intended to counter Warsaw Pact forces. The carriers, based at Toulon, are usually found in the Mediterranean to counter seaborne attacks from the Mediterranean and can be deployed to the Central Atlantic as required. The onboard Aeronavale nuclear-armed component consists of about 15 Super Etendard IV strike aircraft based on each carrier. Each air-

craft is currently armed with a single AN-52 gravity-type nuclear bomb, with a 20-kiloton warhead (as are French Air Force tactical strike aircraft).

Twenty of the Super Etendard IV aircraft are planned for refitting and will be armed with the nuclear-capable Aerospatiale ASMP supersonic "fire and forget" missile. The first compatibility tests with Super Etendard are complete and a number of the aircraft will be refitted by 1990. The French 1984-88 defense program includes one nuclear-powered aircraft carrier (porte aeronefs nucleaire-PAN), which is being built by the DCN firm at the Brest Naval Dockyard.

While the French fleet is primarily concentrated in the Mediterranean, it has major responsibilities for protecting French interests overseas (outre-mer). This includes interests in the Indian Ocean -- centered at Djibouti, Reunion and Mayotte Islands -- which normally includes a flagship and/or replenishment ship, five destroyer/frigates, some coastal minesweepers and auxiliary ships. In late 1987, the French moved one of the Clemenceau class carriers to the northeast Indian Ocean (Arabian Sea), as a direct result of Iranian attacks on tankers and merchant ships in the Persian Gulf.

France also has major interests in the Pacific Basin, largely based on New Caledonia and in the Tahiti Islands (based at Papette), the latter supporting the French nuclear testing program. The ability to deploy an aircraft carrier with embarked strike and surveillance aircraft onboard to these regions adds much to French foreign policies in these outer regions. Thus, the French aircraft carriers perform many of the same roles and support the same type of foreign policies as do the U.S. Navy's super carriers.

The two French conventionally-powered aircraft carriers were the first to be designed as such, built from the keel up and completed in France. France had operated converted vessels and received ex-U.S. Navy and British aircraft carriers in the 1950s, as part of its participation then in NATO. CLEMENCEAU was ordered from the Brest Dockyard on May 28, 1954 and was laid down in November 1955. FOCH was ordered from Chantiers de l'Atlantique at St. Nazaire (Penhoet-loire). FOCH would be initially built at a special dry dock and later completed at the Brest Dockyard. Both carriers were ordered to replace two ex-U.S. Navy DVLs then in Aeronavale service.

CLEMENCEAU (R 98) was commissioned on November 22, 1961, FOCH

(R 99) following on July 15, 1963. When first deployed, their onboard Aeronavale aircraft types were largely as they are today: Crusader interceptors, Etendard strike aircraft and Breguet 1150 Alize single-engined antisubmarine warfare (ASW) aircraft, with two or three light helicopters (SE.313B Alouette II or SA.316B Alouette III) for liaison work. Some logistics support is occasionally provided by the SA.321 Super Frelon heavy helicopter, normally used as a trooping heavy helicopter for French Commandos. The French Navy does not deploy ASW helicopters on its carriers, these being reserved for deployment onboard destroyers and frigates of the fleet.

CLEMENCEAU and FOCH have been periodically overhauled during their careers. CLEMENCEAU was refitted in 1978 to accommodate the new Super Etendard IV strike aircraft then being procured, providing the carrier with a nuclear strike capability for the first time. FOCH had a similar refit from July 1980 to August 1981. CLEMENCEAU

began its next one-year overhaul in September 1985; FOCH is scheduled to emerge from a current overhaul later this year. CLEMENCEAU is scheduled to remain in service until mid-1995, and then be replaced by the first French nuclear-powered carrier (RICHELEAU). FOCH will remain in service until 1998. A second Richeleau class CVN is scheduled for ordering under the 1988-1992 defense plan, which will replace the carrier FOCH.

The two carriers are considerably smaller than current American supercarriers, with two steam catapults and two aircraft lifts. The deck measures 543 x 96.8 feet (165.5 x 29.5 meters) and is angled at eight degrees. The U.S. Kitty Hawk class -- built at the same time -- has a width one-half that of the French carriers' length! Loading the high-performance LTB F-8E (FN) Crusaders thus became a very demanding task on such a small deck.

Close-in defense is now provided by two newly-installed Naval Crotale eight-cell SAM launchers, replacing the for-

mer dozen 3.9-inch (100 mm) automatic guns cited in sponsons, four on each side of the ship. The latter were designed to defeat an aircraft or missile target flying at between Mach 0.9 and 1.2 at altitudes of between 50 and 3,500 meters. Each turret contains a two-axis stabilized Thomson-CSF DRBV 51C (J-band) fire control radar and eight launcher cells. The Matra-built missiles use solid fuel rocket motors, can reach a speed of approximately 800 meters/sec. in 2.3 seconds after launch to a range of about 8.5 kilometers (km). The ships also have SAIGAIE and DAGAIE IR and chaff decoy rocket systems (counterparts to U.S. Navy Super-RBOC).

SUPER ÉTENDARD

CARRYING CAPABILITIES

LOADING CAPABILITY lb		1 000	2 400	1 300	2 400	1 000
AIR TO AIR MISSILES	2 x MATRA 550 Magic					
BOMBS	6 x 250 kg (clean or retarded)					
	4 x 400 kg (clean or retarded)					
ROCKET LAUNCHERS	4 x LR 150 (4 x 18 - 68 mm rockets)					
EXTERNAL FUEL TANKS	1 x 600 l. (160 USG) Drop tank					
	2 x 600 l. (160 USG) Drop tanks					
	2 x 1 100 l. (290 USG) Drop tanks					
AIR TO SEA MISSILE						
BUDDY REFUEL POD						
RECO POD						
CME POD	Active autoprotection (IR or EM) decoy launcher					

At the heart of every aircraft carrier is its embarked airwing. For the French carriers, this comprises about 40 aircraft and two to four utility helicopters. The French Navy has three squadrons (11F, 14F, 17F), each with about 15 Super Etendard IV strike aircraft. Original procurement was planned at 100 aircraft, but was cut for budget reasons to 71 (plus 14 for Argentina). Many of the aircraft are now sporting low-visibility grey colors, replacing the earlier deep blue solid pattern.

The Super Etendard gained initial fame during the Falklands/Malvinas War, flying with the Argentine Air Force. The aircraft is a single-seat strike fighter. Changes were made in the earlier Etendard's wing, contemplated by the need for the aircraft to land onboard with an unexpended Aerospatiale AM.39 EXOCET antiship missile underwing. Maximum catapult launch weight is 26,235 pounds (11,900 kilo-

grams), which is comparatively light by American attack aircraft launch weights. Landing speed is at about 125 knots.

The aircraft is powered by a SNECMA Atar 8K50 (essentially a Mirage F.1s 9K50) with a simple augmented jetpipe and fixed nozzle in place of the afterburner. Rated engine output is 11,025 pounds (5,000 kg). Aircraft maximum speed is up to Mach 1.0 (1,205 km/hr) at 10,000 meters (733 mph at sea level), with a maximum ceiling of about 45,000 feet. The Super Etendard's combat radius, armed with a single AM.39 EXOCET, is 475 nautical miles (800 km) with underwing and belly auxiliary fuel tanks. The AM.39 is carried on the right inboard pylon. Maximum internal fuel capacity is up to 3,270 liters and up to 2,800 additional liters externally.

The small cockpit is reminiscent of the MD A-4 Skyhawk, of which the Super

Etendard has many of the same performance and weapons-carrying abilities. Wingspan is but 9.6 meters (7.8 when folded). Empty weight is 6,500 kg. The pilot is provided with a Thomson-CSF VE 120 head up display (HUD), Crouzet type 97 navigation display, Crouzet 66 air data computer, LMT TACAN, TRT radio altimeter, SFIM three-axis altitude indicator, armament control panel, and weapons selection box. A Sagem-Kearfott ETNA inertial nav and attack system provide for precise distant flying (accurate to 1.2 nautical miles per flight hour). The Thomson-CSF/ESG Agave radar provides search/track/designation/telemetry/ navigation functions for both aircraft and guided weapons. Agave range in the air-to-air search mode is 28 km (15 nm). While in the surface search mode, it is 100 km (60 nm), with bearing sectors up to 140 degrees.

The Super Etendard carries two 30mm DEFA 552A cannons (internal gun pack) with a firing rate of 1,250 rounds per minute. Externally, a wide variety of ordnance can be carried on five attachment points, including the centerline pylon stress for up to 1,300 lbs (590 kg). Typical attack modes would carry six 550-lb (250-kg) bombs, or four 882-lb (400-kg) bombs, or four LR-150 rocket pods, each with 18 Matra 68mm unguided rockets. For antishipping strikes using the AM.39, which is carried on the right inboard pylon, a 242 l. gallon (1,000 liter) tank is carried on the port inboard pylon.

Other optional combinations include an MD Buddy refueling pack, Philips-Matra Phimat chaff pod, and a single free-fall AN 52 nuclear weapon. The Super Etendard was specifically equipped to carry two Matra 550 MAGIC 2 air-to-air missiles (AAMs) for the intercept and self-defense role. With two MAGIC and two external 242 1. gallon fuel tanks, a Hi-Hi radius is 650 nm (2,305 km).

Beginning this year, numbers of Super Etendards entering service will be capable of carrying the Aerospatiale ASMP 100-150 kiloton air-to-surface nuclear weapon, replacing the AN 52 fittings. A total of 53 Super Etendards are being converted to carry the 54 nm (100 km) range standoff ASMP. As with the EXOCET (and other contemporary ASMs), the I-band Agave monopulse radar system feeds pre-launch data to the ASMP. The last 10 refitted aircraft are due for delivery during 1989.

Because of the Super Etendards agile flight characteristics and acceptably low landing speeds, only six aircraft losses had resulted by the beginning of 1986. After the 1990s, Super Etendards may also get the Aerospatiale supersonic ANS antiship missile to replace the AM.39 ANS. This will represent a quantum improvement in speed and maneuverability over the EXOCET, greatly improving kill probabilities (pk) against Soviet Mediterranean-operating warships in event of a major East-West conflict. Super Etendards are unlikely to be built again without a major war involving French military forces. Replacements still could be obtained, as Dassault offered in 1985 to re-open the production line if sufficient orders -- how many unspecified -- could be obtained. That has yet to occur and Aeronavale is already undertaking Rafale carrier-suitability RDT&E with the aim of naval Rafales being used onboard the future Richeleau class CVNs.

Scenes of life aboard the French aircraft carrier, FOCH, on the high seas -- (clockwise from top left) -- ship's commander checks activities on deck; aircraft are stowed and serviced below deck; a view of the machine room; personnel review deck techniques for launching and retrieval of aircraft using models of the Super Etendard.

F-8E (FN) CRUSADER

The French carriers each carry a squadron-equivalent flight of F-8E (FN) Crusader interceptors. When first entering service nearly 25 years ago, the Aeronavale Crusaders were state-of-the-art gunfighters! The French Navy production run, consisting of 4,212 single-seat modified F-8Es, have remained as interceptor aircraft, as no strike capability has been added.

Powerplant for the aircraft is a Pratt & Whitney J57-P-20A delivering 18,000 lbs of thrust with afterburning, providing the aircraft with a maximum speed of 943 knots (Mach 1.8). The French originally ordered 40 single-seaters and six TF-8A two-seat trainers. The U.S. Congress cancelled the two-seat aircraft program for the U.S. Navy, resulting in a revised French order for 42 single-seaters and spares. The last Dallas-built F-8E (FN) was completed in January 1965.

A major winning feature of the Crusader was its small size and ability to operate from the small French carriers. Empty weight is about 28,000 lbs, making it the heaviest aircraft operating onboard the carriers. The only drawback was the aircraft's 113- knot landing speed -- considered too hot for such short deck space! The Vought engineers changed the wing's camber (doubling it), enlarged the entire tailplane for better handling, and designed a boundary layer control system which blew air through nozzles mounted in the wing across the flaps and ailerons, creating added airflow and lift at low speeds. Today, Aeronavale Crusaders can come screaming across the fantail at about 90 knots landing speed!

Crusaders carry four internal 20mm cannon (84 rds/gun), two to four early-model AIM-9 SIDEWINDERs, or two Matra 530D long-range AAMs. An AN/AAS-15 infrared scanner is installed in the front of the windscreen for more accurate AIM-9 missile control. The Matra 530D is a heavyweight AAM, intended for long-range bomber or cruise missile intercepts. More recently, F-8Es (FNs) are reportedly modified to also carry Matra 550 MAGIC-series short-range dogfight AAMs. Endurance is about two hours, with a combat radius of 680 nm.

French carriers carry a flight of Breguet Alize ASW aircraft, 75 of which were built for Aeronavale. All were rebuilt in recent years to extend their service life. The aircraft has a four to seven hour endurance, with a maximum speed of about 285 mph (459 km) at sea level. Alizes have an internal weapons bay for ASW torpedoes, bombs or depth charges. For the light attack role, six underwing pylons can be used for bombs or unguided rockets. The bulged wing nacelles contain sonobuoys.

Periodic visitors to the French carriers are optical reconnaissance Etendard IV-P aircraft of a single shore-based squadron. These also operate as a buddy-pack refueling aircraft for Super Etendards or Crusaders, and each retains two 20mm DEFA cannon (and can carry two AIM-9s and up to 3,000 lbs of external ordnance). Three French Omera optical cameras are carried in the nose, plus two in a ventral position. The aircraft provide much the same photo reconnaissance capability as did U.S. Navy RF-8 Crusaders. Etendard IV-Ps are operated on the carriers as operational assignments may require.

With increased cooperation between France and NATO, particularly in the Mediterranean, France's two aircraft carriers represent an important part of Western naval forces in the European theater. They will gain increasing firepower by 1990, as new antiship and land-attack missiles are added to existing aircraft. They are also a significant part of French naval power designed to deal with conventional war threats -- aimed at either former colonies or its own soil. [D]

EVOLVING NAVAL TECHNOLOGY

HIGHER, FASTER, FARTHER, DEEPER

by Philip Farris

As the U.S. Navy comes within hailing distance of the 21st century, it finds itself challenged around the globe by the Soviet Union's blue water Navy.
Today, the Navy world is the whole world -- land, sea, beneath the sea and in the air.

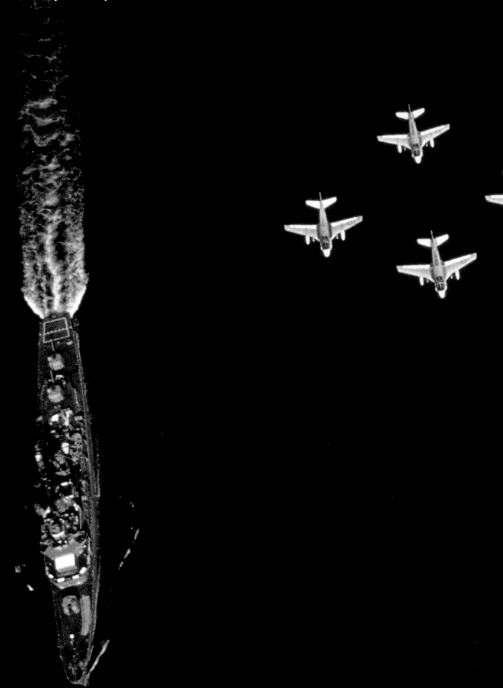

Aircraft from the aircraft carrier USS AMERICA (CV-66) as they fly over ships assigned to the America Task Group in the Atlantic Ocean.

The role of seapower in the life of the United States has remained consistent since 1776. Throughout the years, the fleet has been used as a deterrent to war, as a diplomatic signal in steps short of war, or in war itself. In recent times, naval operations have taken place in the Persian Gulf and in the central Mediterranean -- the latter to demonstrate "freedom of navigation" in and near waters claimed by Libya but recognized virtually by all nations as international.

As in the past, the U.S. Navy is ready to carry out its mission. Its size and composition make it the perfect instrument for executing our national and maritime strategies. As Admiral Carlisle A.H. Trost, Chief of Naval Operations, said recently: "It exploits our advantages in geography, technology, experience, and training -- and our adversaries' disadvantages in those same areas."

The Navy has certain features that make it unique among fighting forces. It is on station 24 hours a day, never far from the scene of a potential crisis. It is entirely flexible. When one mission is completed, the ships and aircraft are ready for another. Admiral Trost has pointed out that "there is no pausing to regroup."

Another feature of the Navy is that it operates in international waters, where no government's permission is required to base and fly aircraft. At the same time, its ships, in a perfectly legal way, can signal menace to any potential troublemaker. Lastly, the Navy is both self-sufficient and interoperable. Ships on station carry with them enough supplies to sustain them for at least two months. Whatever they need from ashore can be brought to them by the combat logistics ships and transferred at sea.

Today's Navy comprises some 570 ships, with that number expected to grow by 1989. The centerpiece of the fleet is the force of 15 large-deck aircraft carriers which, in company with cruisers, destroyers, and frigates, as well as combat logistics ships and shore-based maritime patrol aircraft, provide the United States its naval striking power.

In addition to operating in support of the carrier battle groups, attack submarines conduct independent surveillance patrols. "Fleet ballistic missile submarines," the Chief of Naval Operations points out, "constitute the most survivable leg of our strategic triad of nuclear deterrence."

Amphibious ships carry a different kind of offensive power -- the men and equipment of the U.S. Marine Corps, elite assault forces. Also in the fleet are the mine countermeasures ships, missile-equipped patrol hydrofoils, and salvage, repair and other support ships that go with the fleet.

As it prepares for the challenges of the future, the U.S. Navy is retaining and using functional technologies which are still doing the job, while melding the old with new technologies to build the fleet America needs. A good example of this is the new Ticonderoga class cruiser. The USS TICONDEROGA (CG-47) was the first in this new class of guided missile cruisers that carries the AEGIS weapons systems -- the most advanced air defense system in the world today.

The development of TOMAHAWK, HARPOON and AEGIS is changing the traditional defensive role of the surface Navy. In addition to providing important antiship offensive capability, TOMAHAWK and HARPOON now give the Navy the ability to attack land targets at extended range -- a new dimension in surface warfare. AEGIS -- the shield -- provides unequalled defensive and offensive capabilities.

Over the last 200 years, and more, U.S. Navy ships have advanced from sail to steam, then to nuclear power and gas turbines. Hulls have evolved from wood to steel, aluminum and glass reinforced plastic. Their shapes, however, have generally remained the same -- a single long monohull. Due to its inherent hydrodynamic benefits, this shape will continue as the backbone of the surface fleet into the next century. But, new and exciting "alternative hull forms" have already begun to enter the fleet.

New technologies notwithstanding, "the fleet of the future will be in many respects similar to today's fleet," says Admiral Trost. In his view, it will include both large and small ships -- ranging from fleet ballistic missile submarines to a broad spectrum of surface vessels. He sees a continued upgrading, in particular, of the Navy's antisubmarine warfare (ASW) capabilities. This is necessary to carry out the mission of protecting and controlling the sea lines of communication from the Soviet submarine menace.

Chief of Naval Operations Trost has provided a telling illustration of how the naval warfare "envelope" has expanded exponentially in recent years. He has pointed out that "in the last 10 years alone the 'envelope' that used to measure 20-30 miles on the surface, by 40,000 - 60,000 feet in the air, by 400 feet below, now extends several hundred miles into space, and all the way down to the ocean floor."

The aircraft and ships of the U.S. Navy, some of which are shown on these pages, have extended the "envelope" dramatically. They ensure the root strength of our seapower and the world leadership we must retain. For the future, Navy technology will continue to push higher, faster, farther, and deeper.

THE AMPHIBIOUS NAVY

"Getting There First With The Most..."

by Kirby J. Harrison

In 1969, a new ship joined the amphibious Navy. As she slipped into her berth at the Naval Amphibious Base at Little Creek, Virginia, she was a subject for discussion and occasional laughter. To the old amphibious sailor, she looked like nothing he had ever seen.

Her stern was squared and hung with a huge ramp down to the waterline. Her main deck towered nearly 40 feet above the water and, amidships, her sides extended upward another six levels. From fore to aft, the length of the superstructure was a tunnel connecting the forward and after main deck.

Strangest of all was the bow, where two great derrick arms projected from the main deck like gigantic bowsprits. The derricks were part of an even more unusual arrangement that allowed for extension of a 112-foot ramp to permit vehicles to roll ashore from either the beached ship or to a floating causeway reaching the shore.

She was the USS NEWPORT, first of a new tank landing ship class (LST) and she signaled the birth of the new, 20-knot, amphibious Navy.

The NEWPORT was a radical departure from the old bow-door design developed by the British in World War II. The need for speed was not compatible with bow-door construction, so the NEWPORT's engineers came up with a "clam shell" door that would open up the forepeak at a point well above the waterline. This would expose the vehicle ramp, which could then be extended and lowered by two derrick cranes extending at an angle from either side of the doors. It may have looked strange, but it worked.

Now the amphibious Navy had an LST that would make better than 20 knots, yet still draw less than 12 feet of water fully loaded, and that could pull up close to a beach to disgorge her landing party. If necessary, she could even stand off the beach, lower from her sides huge floating causeway modules and, in a matter of hours, construct a floating bridge from the anchored vessel to shore.

In her lower tank deck, she could carry Marine Corps amphibious tracked landing vehicles, tanks, and supplies. By flooding wing tanks on either side of the ship, the tank deck could be submerged to take aboard the newest 135-foot long utility landing craft.

Five hundred and twenty-two feet long and 8,450 tons, she could embark with and put ashore a complement of 400 Marines with full equipment.

Within three years after the NEWPORT was commissioned, 19 more ships of her class were on active service. In that same time period, 24 more amphibious ships were commissioned: five Anchorage class dock landing ships (LSDs); 11 Austin class and the first of two Raleigh class amphibious transport docks (LPDs); all five Charleston class amphibious cargo ships (LKAs); and the BLUE RIDGE and MT. WHITNEY, state- of-the-art amphibious command ships (LCCs).

By 1972, seven Marine helicopter- carrying amphibious assault ships (LPHs) were in service, advancing the concept of aerial assault as part of an amphibious operation. Additionally, construction had begun on the first two of five Tarawa class multi-purpose amphibious assault ships (LHAs), to combine the idea of helicopter assault with other amphibious operations.

In less than five years, an amphibious Navy that had rusted in a backwater of 25 years of benign neglect was well on its way to becoming what planners had hoped for -- a "gator" force that could take advantage of new technology and take its place in a new, modern Navy.

If technology has changed the look and application of things, the strategy of an amphibious assault has remained basically the same. Get there first with the most, put it ashore and support it!

At the Naval Amphibious School in Little Creek, they teach the concept more formally. Says a former instructor, "The idea is to surprise the opposition, neutralize adversary firepower, put the landing party ashore safely, and support them afterward."

In 1983, the Navy embarked on an ambitious new program called "The Department of the Navy Long Term Amphibious Lift Requirement and Optimum Ship Mix Study," thankfully shortened to "Amphibious Lift."

The objective was to increase the amphibious lift capability to include assault echelons of the Marine Amphibious Force and a Marine Amphibious Brigade. Previous lift ability was limited to a Marine Amphibious Force. Inclusion of an entire amphibious brigade would mean an increase of a full one-third.

The solution is already off the planning board. In fact, parts of it are deployed and the remainder will be operational by 1990.

The dock landing ship WHIDBEY ISLAND joined the fleet in 1985 and two more sister ships, the GERMANTOWN and FORT McHENRY, followed in 1986 and 1987. Three more of this "cargo variant" LSD are planned as part of the Amphibious Lift program. A second element of the Amphibious Lift concept is construction of the new LHD class amphibious assault ship. The lead ship, the USS WASP, was launched in September and is scheduled for commissioning in mid-1989.

According to amphibious experts, the new helicopter-carrying ship is a "...better thought-out concept" than the previous LHA class. While the multirole ship seemed a good idea from a cost point of view, it turned out to be less practical. The requirements for the various roles often conflicted, so that the ship was frequently restricted to carrying out a single mission.

The LHD ship will correct that. While taking advantage of her combat information center to direct an amphibious operation from a position out of range of shore-based weapons, she will be able to launch aircraft and landing craft simultaneously in support of the landing force.

The third element in the Amphibious Lift program brings all three together. It is the long-awaited surface effect landing craft, officially designated an LCAC, or landing craft air cushion.

Both the LSD-41 class and the LHD class will be capable of carrying these big, fast assault craft, and launching them with their Marine Corps assault units from positions "over the horizon" and out of range of shore weapons. The older, much slower, diesel-powered utility landing craft and even slower mechanized landing craft could have been launched from positions over the horizon, but stood little chance of avoiding shore directed fire on the long, slow trip to the beach.

The 170-ton (loaded) LCAC has a range of more than 200 miles and skims over the water at speeds in excess of 40 knots. Even with a full load of 25 Marines and their equipment, it is able to negotiate difficult beach landings more easily than the old landing craft with the big bow doors.

The amphibious Navy is enthusiastic enough about this exotic landing craft that they have ensured a fiscal year 1988 budget request of $43.7 million for advance procurement of materials for the fiscal year 1989 building program. Twelve of these air cushion craft have already been delivered, 21 are under contract and, as of 1986, a total of 33 have been authorized.

Also very high on the list of priorities in the next decade is continued development of the V-22 Osprey tilt-rotor aircraft. This innovative aircraft has an engine/transmission mounted on each wingtip. Operating as a helicopter with the engine nacelles rotated upward, it easily takes off and lands vertically. Once airborne, the nacelles are rotated forward as much as 90 degrees for high-speed horizontal flight.

As a vertical assault vehicle, the Marine Corps is looking forward to its arrival sometime in 1991.

With the increased capabilities of the LHD, LHA, LPH, and new LSD-41 classes to operate effectively with the Marine Corps AV-8B Harrier VSTOL jet, the armed-to-the-teeth Cobra attack heli-copter, and the future V-22 Osprey, the ability of the amphibious Navy to do its job is greatly enhanced.

As the amphibious Navy has grown in numbers and technology, it has also learned valuable lessons in strategy in places like Lebanon and Grenada.

According to one amphibious expert, "Maybe the most important thing we learned from the Lebanon and Grenada experience was that we must work more efficiently as a team during joint services operations."

With this in mind, and over the protests of some, Joint Interoperability of Tactical Command and Control Systems (JINTACCS) is being developed. The somewhat unwieldy acronym is short for a new joint services message format that will enable members of the various services to "speak" the same "language" when they communicate.

If the future of the "gator" Navy looks bright, it is in no small part because many of those in the amphibious force remember too well the years of neglect after World War II. They are determined that by planning ahead and making use of new technology they will be ready.

U.S. maritime strategists speculate that in the years to come there will be increasing numbers of relatively small, conventional conflicts in places far removed from the United States.

A ready amphibious force will have to play a major role in a 600-ship Navy to ensure the success of that strategy. ∎